The History of College Nicknames, Mascots and School Colors

The History of College Nicknames, Mascots and School Colors

GARY HUDSON

ISBN:	Hardcover	978-1-7960-7256-3
	Softcover	978-1-7960-7255-6
	eBook	978-1-7960-7257-0

Print information available on the last page.

Rev. date: 11/22/2019

To order additional copies of this book, contact:
Xlibris
1-888-795-4274
www.Xlibris.com
Orders@Xlibris.com
803166

CONTENTS

Acknowledgements ix

Appalachian State University 1
Arizona State University 2
Arkansas State University 3
Auburn University 5
Ball State University 7
Baylor University 8
Boise State University 9
Boston College 10
Bowling Green State University 11
Brigham Young University 12
Central Michigan University 13
Clemson University 14
Coastal Carolina University..15
Colorado State University...16
Duke University...17
East Carolina University...19
Eastern Michigan University 20
Florida Atlantic University 21
Florida International University 22
Florida State University... 23
Fresno State University.. 24
Georgia Institute of Technology 25
Georgia Southern University 26
Georgia State University.. 27
Indiana University 28
Iowa State University... 29
Kansas State University..31

Kent State University...32
Liberty University...33
Louisiana State University.. 34
Louisiana Tech University...35
Marshall University 36
Miami University...37
Michigan State University 38
Middle Tennessee State University..39
Mississippi State University 40
New Mexico State University..41
North Carolina State University 42
Northern Illinois University... 44
Northwestern University..45
Ohio State University... 46
Ohio University...47
Oklahoma State University.. 49
Old Dominion University 50
Oregon State University...51
Pennsylvania State University 52
Purdue University 53
Rice University 54
Rutgers University 55
San Diego State University.. 56
San Jose State University.. 58
Southern Methodist University... 59
Stanford University.. 60
Syracuse University 61
Temple University.. 63
Texas A&M University.. 64
Texas Christian University 65
Texas State University–San Marcos 66
Texas Tech University...67
Troy University 68
Tulane University... 69
United States Air Force Academy 70
United States Military Academy 71
United States Naval Academy 72
University of Akron.. 73

University of Alabama...74
University of Alabama at Birmingham 76
University of Arizona 77
University of Arkansas 78
University of Buffalo 79
University of California at Berkeley...80
University of California at Los Angeles...81
University of Central Florida 82
University of Cincinnati...83
University of Colorado..84
University of Connecticut..85
University of Florida...86
University of Georgia 88
University of Hawaii...89
University of Houston...91
University of Illinois 92
University of Iowa..93
University of Kansas..94
University of Kentucky 96
University of Louisiana–Lafayette 97
University of Louisville 98
University of Louisiana at Monroe..99
University of Maryland...100
University of Massachusetts–Amherst...101
University of Memphis 102
University of Miami...103
University of Michigan...104
University of Minnesota 106
University of Mississippi 107
University of Missouri...109
University of Nebraska 110
University of Nevada at Las Vegas..111
University of Nevada at Reno...112
University of New Mexico..113
University of North Carolina–Chapel Hill 115
University of North Carolina–Charlotte...116
University of North Texas..117
University of Notre Dame..118

University of Oklahoma...120
University of Oregon 121
University of Pittsburgh..122
University of South Alabama...123
University of South Carolina 124
University of South Florida...125
University of Southern California 126
University of Southern Mississippi...128
University of Tennessee 130
University of Texas 131
University of Texas at El Paso 132
University of Texas at San Antonio 133
University of Toledo..134
University of Tulsa..135
University of Utah...136
University of Virginia..137
University of Washington 138
University of Wisconsin..140
University of Wyoming...141
Utah State University..142
Vanderbilt University..143
Virginia Polytechnic Institute and State University.............................144
Wake Forest University...145
Washington State University 146
West Virginia University 148
Western Kentucky University..149
Western Michigan University 150

School Trivia Questions..151

ACKNOWLEDGEMENTS

I would like to thank the following people who inspired and assisted me, in writing my book:

My Sister-In- Law Joy, for convincing me to write this book; the staff at all of the college and universities, that provided me with my requested information needed in order for me to complete my book; my Cousin Bridget, for doing the initial editing for my book; and my Cousin Byron, for informing me about Xlibris, which is the name of the company that published this book.

SCHOOL NAME:	Appalachian State University
NICKNAME:	Mountaineers
MASCOT:	mountaineer ("Yosef")
COLORS:	black and gold
CONFERENCE:	Sun Belt Conference

HISTORY

The official nickname for Appalachian State University (ASU) athletic teams is the Mountaineers.

The official mascot for Appalachian State University athletic teams is Yosef. The expression "Yosef" is a mountain talk slang word that means "yourself." Therefore, if you are a graduate of ASU or a fan and have a heart that is composed of black and gold, you are, in fact, Yosef. Yosef was created by James Storie and Elizabeth South (editors of ASU's yearbook called the *Rhododendron*) and Lloyd S. Isaacs and Bill Mitchell (of the Observer Publishing Company). He was originally created as a fictional character named Dan'l Boone Yoseff from Appalachian and as a member of the 1941–42 freshman class. Yoseff was an instant hit with ASU students, but there was controversy about who actually created his image. From 1946 to 1949, Yoseff reappeared as a guest editorial writer in ASU's student newspaper, the *Appalachian*. His writings focused on popular mountain expressions and misspelled words. In January 1947, the second f in his name was removed. Yosef was first considered as ASU's mascot in the *Appalachian* on March 12, 1948, when a photograph was taken of him as a returning freshman. In 1949, John Geffrich became one of the first people to portray Yosef as a mascot.

ASU's official school colors are black and gold. Unfortunately, there is no historical data explaining why those colors were chosen.

SCHOOL NAME:	Arizona State University
NICKNAME:	Sun Devils
MASCOT:	sun devil ("Sparky")
COLORS:	maroon and gold
CONFERENCE:	Pacific 12 Conference

HISTORY

Prior to being named Arizona State University (ASU), the school was called Tempe Normal, and the school nickname was the Owls. That name was chosen by the 1889 football team. Then when the school name changed to the Arizona State Teachers College, the new nickname became the Bulldogs. The school chose that name because Yale and other schools of notoriety were nicknamed the Bulldogs, so the Teachers College chose that name in an effort to achieve a higher level of respect. In 1946, when the school name was changed to Arizona State University, the *State Press*, which was ASU's school newspaper, frequently appealed to have the nickname changed to the Sun Devils. When the student body voted on November 20, 1946, to have the name changed, the result was 819–196, in favor of Sun Devils. The name Sun Devil was heard for the first time when somebody shouted it in a crowd. That person's identity was never determined.

In 1948, Sparky the Red Devil became ASU's official mascot. Sparky, a costumed red devil with a pitchfork, was created by Berk Anthony, who was an illustrator and former employee of Walt Disney. Rumor has it that Anthony derived Sparky's facial features from his former boss.

Maroon and gold are the official school colors for ASU athletic teams. Gold was chosen in 1896 because it signifies ASU's "golden promise," which is to ensure that every student receives a valuable educational experience. Gold also signifies Arizona's sunshine, its power, and the influence it has on the state's climate and economy. In 1898, maroon became the other official color. Maroon signifies sacrifice and bravery.

SCHOOL NAME: Arkansas State University
NICKNAME: Red Wolves
MASCOT: wolves ("How" and "Scarlet")
COLORS: scarlet and black
CONFERENCE: Sun Belt Conference

HISTORY

From 1911 to 1931, Arkansas State University (ASU) officials made a conscious effort to select a suitable nickname for the university. ASU was first called the Aggies (short for "agriculture") or the Farmers, since it was the only agricultural school in Eastern Arkansas. Then in 1925, the nickname Gorillas started to be used. But that name proved to be very unpopular. Finally, in 1930, ASU got on track and called their athletic teams the Warriors, which eventually evolved to the Indians one year later. The Indians were chosen as ASU's official nickname to honor the vast amount of Indian tribes, the Osage tribe in particular, which once roamed throughout the state of Arkansas prior to the arrival of the settlers. The Osage tribe, which lived in the northern part of Arkansas in the eighteenth century, was at war with just about all the other Indian tribes that occupied the state. Their fighting Indian spirit is the reason ASU officials chose the Indians as the nickname to represent the school's athletic teams. On January 31, 2008, ASU's Mascot Selection Committee unanimously decided that the school nickname needed to be changed to the Red Wolves. So they made that recommendation to the school's chancellor, Dr. Robert Potts. Dr. Potts agreed, and the NCAA approved the name change on March 7, 2008. The phasing out of the Indians nickname also involved the football stadium name being changed from Indian Stadium to ASU Stadium. In 2012 and 2015, the stadium name was changed to Liberty Bank Stadium and Centennial Bank Stadium, respectively.

In an effort to choose a mascot that would be directly related to the ASU nickname, the Indian family was chosen. The Indian family, which is a trio of ASU students made up in Indian attire, is led by Chief Big Track

3

(named after the chief of the Osage tribe), who is the head of the family, an unnamed princess, and an unnamed brave. On January 31, 2008, the Mascot Selection Committee also decided to select the Wolves as ASU's new school mascot. Two wolves were selected, and the names given to them were How and Scarlet.

Besides 1911 being the first year that football was introduced at ASU, an ASU committee made up of several students and one faculty member chose scarlet and black as the official school colors to represent its athletic teams. In doing so, the first use of the official colors was on the school's pennant.

SCHOOL NAME:	Auburn University
NICKNAME:	Tigers
MASCOT:	golden eagle ("Tiger")
COLORS:	burnt orange and navy blue
CONFERENCE:	Southeastern Conference

HISTORY

For years, college sports fans have incorrectly chanted, yelled, and often referred to Auburn University (AU) athletic teams by the wrong nickname. Many people incorrectly call AU teams the War Eagles or Plainsmen, and for good reason. Auburn does, in fact, have an eagle as a mascot. This is where the confusion should end. To set the record straight, AU teams are nicknamed the Tigers. The idea of this nickname came about when an AU student or faculty member saw a line from an Oliver Goldsmith poem that read, "Where crouching tigers wait their hopeless prey . . ." Goldsmith, of course, is a well-known figure to all AU students and faculty for his infamous poem titled "Sweet Auburn." Get the connection? Furthermore, the term "plainsmen" was, in fact, derived from a line in the "Sweet Auburn" poem. It read, "Sweet Auburn, loveliest village of the plain . . ." Since Auburn athletes were from the plains in the early days, they were often nicknamed the Plainsmen.

Auburn University's famous "War Eagle!" cheer is the catalyst why the school mascot is an eagle. And although the origin of the cheer is anyone's guess, there are several stories that claim to support the mascot's existence. The name Tiger was given to AU's golden eagle mascot because of the name being synonymous with the school's nickname.

Like the origin of Auburn University's golden eagle mascot, there is also no concrete evidence to support the origin of AU's colors. However, until otherwise proven, there is one possible theory. When Auburn University was first established in 1856, it was called East Alabama

Male College. The man responsible for relocating the school to Auburn, Alabama, was a gentleman by the name of Reverend O. R. Blue. It's very possible that AU's orange and blue colors were chosen by AU's student body or staff to honor O. R. Blue.

SCHOOL NAME:	Ball State University
NICKNAME:	Cardinals
MASCOT:	cardinal ("Charlie")
COLORS:	cardinal red and white
CONFERENCE:	Mid-American Conference

HISTORY

In 1927, the *Easterner,* Ball State University's school newspaper, was prompted by administrators, coaches, and students to sponsor a contest to determine a new school nickname. This was due to them being dissatisfied with the current nickname, Hoosieroons. In doing so, the newspaper offered five dollars in gold for the selected suggestion. Dissatisfied with the names that were submitted, the committee decided that they could find a better name themselves. One week later, while two of the committee members, Prof. Billy Paul Williams and Coach Norman G. Wann, were discussing possible names, Williams, who was a St. Louis Cardinals baseball fan, commented on how much he liked the cardinal insignia on Roger Hornsby's sweatshirt. At that moment, he decided to submit the name to the committee. When the committee members presented the name to the students, a vote was conducted, and on November 30, Cardinals was chosen as the new official nickname for Ball State University. Needless to say, Professor Williams won the five-dollar gold prize.

In 1969, Charlie Cardinal made his debut as the official mascot for Ball State University.

Since the Cardinals was Ball State University's nickname, cardinal red seemed like a natural choice for the official color of the school's athletic teams. White was added as a background color.

SCHOOL NAME:	Baylor University
NICKNAME:	Bears
MASCOT:	bear
COLORS:	green and gold
CONFERENCE:	Big 12 Conference

HISTORY

After seventy years of not having a school nickname or mascot, the students at Baylor University decided to hold a contest in 1914 to put an end to their long and much-needed quest. After voting via ballot that included twelve possible choices, the bear was selected as the official nickname and mascot for Baylor University.

The selection of Baylor University's official school colors happened during the spring of 1897 in a very unique and unplanned way. While on a train ride to Bryan, Texas, for a debate team competition, a Baylor University student, who was also a member of the university's school color selection committee, was captured by the beauty of the green and yellow color combination of a sea of dandelions he saw from his train window. Other committee members that were also present on the train agreed and decided to take further action once they returned to Waco. After returning from their trip, the selection committee chose green and opted to go with gold instead of yellow to represent Baylor University and its athletic teams.

SCHOOL NAME: Boise State University
NICKNAME: Broncos
MASCOT: bronco
COLORS: blue and orange
CONFERENCE: Mountain West Conference

HISTORY

In 1932, both the school mascot and colors were selected when Boise State University was founded. A group of students recommended the bronco to be the mascot and then selected blue and orange as the colors. Each selection was approved by a vote with the student body. Blue and orange were selected because no other Idaho institution was using that color scheme at the time. The bronco was selected to reflect the small-town Western flavor of the campus and surrounding communities.

SCHOOL NAME:	Boston College
NICKNAME:	Eagles
MASCOT:	eagle
COLORS:	maroon and gold
CONFERENCE:	Atlantic Coast Conference

HISTORY

In 1920, the eagle became the official mascot and nickname for Boston College (BC), thanks to a man by the name of Rev. Edward McLaughlin. He firmly believed that a mascot would enhance school spirit and pride. Furthermore, the one mascot that he felt would best represent this philosophy would be the eagle, because it symbolizes greatest and dignity, power and freedom.

From the time Boston College was first established in 1863 until the mid-1880s, BC athletic teams have had no school colors or other visual aid for students to proclaim where their loyalties lie. A student committee was formed and led by T. J. Hurley (composer of the school songs "For Boston" and the "Alma Mater") to determine which school colors would best represent Boston College. After considering using the colors of school rivals Holy Cross (purple), Fordham (maroon), and Georgetown (blue and gray), the committee unanimously decided to select maroon and gold as the school's official colors.

SCHOOL NAME: Bowling Green State University
NICKNAME: Falcons
MASCOT: falcon ("Freddie and Frieda")
COLORS: brown and orange
CONFERENCE: Mid-American Conference

HISTORY

Before Bowling Green State University (BGSU) took its name in 1927. It was an institution well known for its teachers training curriculum. The name of the school was formally Bowling Green Normal University, and its athletic teams were nicknamed the Normals. When the name of the school was changed in 1927, a man by the name of Doc Lake, who was a 1923 distinguished graduate of Normal University and an active athletic booster of the new BGSU, suggested that the school's nickname be changed as well. Doc, who was now a sports reporter for the local *Sentinel Tribune* newspaper, got the idea of incorporating a school mascot and changing the school nickname to the Falcons after reading an article about falconry. Because a falcon is a fierce fighting bird with speed and courage, he felt it would be the perfect mascot to represent Bowling Green's athletic teams. To his delight, his suggestion was approved by the school's administration, and the Falcons were officially adopted as the nickname and mascot for Bowling Green State University.

In 1914, Dr. Williams, BGSU's first president, organized a committee that included Dr. L. L. Winslow, from the Industrial Arts Department, to help select new school colors for BGSU. While on a trolley ride to Toledo, Dr. Winslow was sitting behind a lady who was wearing a large hat that had beautiful brown and orange feathers. This gave him inspiration. Dr. Winslow went back to BGSU and convinced the other committee members to approve the orange and brown color combination as the new school colors.

SCHOOL NAME: Brigham Young University
NICKNAME: Cougars
MASCOT: cougar ("Cosmo")
COLORS: blue and white
CONFERENCE: Division I FBS Independents

HISTORY

Brigham Young University (BYU) chose the Cougar nickname to represent all their athletic teams because it is an animal native to the state of Utah. The nickname was first introduced by Eugene L. Roberts in the 1920s. Mr. Roberts was head of the Physical Education Department at BYU. This nickname was also chosen because the cougar embodies the strength and majesty of a lion, the symbol of kings, the speed of a cheetah, the symbol of a ruler, the beauty of a Leopard, and the cunning of a panther. In 1924, only BYU's football team was called the Cougars. Then in the 1950s, all BYU athletic teams were given that name.

In 1923, David Rust, who was a BYU alumnus and a tour guide on the Colorado River, captured a mother cougar and her two kittens. He named the kittens Cleo and Tarbo and brought them to BYU to be used as mascots. The kittens were kept in a cage close to where the present-day stadium is located. Then in 1929, Cleo and Tarbo escaped and terrorized the city of Provo. In 1930, Cleo died, and Tarbo was left to carry on his duties as BYU's mascot. Once all of BYU's athletic teams were given the Cougar nickname, the university decided that its teams would be better represented by a costumed cougar as opposed to a live animal. Because of that, Dwayne Stevenson, who was the pep chairman of BYU, created Cosmo the Cougar, who made his first appearance on October 15, 1953.

Although there is no documentation that clearly explains why BYU uses the colors blue and white, it is believed that those two colors were chosen as the official school colors because blue represents truth and white represents purity.

SCHOOL NAME: Central Michigan University
NICKNAME: Chippewas
MASCOT: none
COLORS: maroon and gold
CONFERENCE: Mid-American Conference

HISTORY

The official nickname for Central Michigan University (CMU) athletic teams is the Chippewas. In 1942, Doc Sewwney, who was the assistant football coach, suggested that the Chippewas replace the current Bearcats nickname, because bearcats had nothing to do with the school or the area and were an extinct animal that no one had ever heard of or seen. The Chippewa name is associated with the name of CMU's yearbook, the Chippewa River that flows through Mount Pleasant (CMU's town), and the Chippewa Indian tribe that once inhabited the area. Therefore, the Chippewa name represents pride and tradition for the band and CMU athletic teams. The new nickname was selected in a student body vote in 1942.

Although members of the Chippewa Indian tribe have given CMU permission to use Chippewas as the nickname, members of the tribe are against the use of their image as a mascot because it reflects a negative meaning toward their culture and heritage. It is for this reason that CMU does not have an official mascot.

In 1924, CMU's student body took a vote to select the official school colors for their athletic teams. At the conclusion of that vote, the colors maroon and gold were selected.

SCHOOL NAME: Clemson University
NICKNAME: Tigers
MASCOT: "the Tiger"
COLORS: orange and purple
CONFERENCE: Atlantic Coast Conference

HISTORY

In 1896, Walter Merritt Riggs, who formed Clemson's first football team, came from Agricultural and Mechanical College of Alabama (later renamed Auburn University). When he came to Clemson, he also decided to take a lot of his former university's ideas with him. At that time, Clemson was low on funds and resources, so Riggs decided to borrow some of Auburn University's old practice uniforms and give them to the Clemson football team. Navy blue and orange were Auburn's school colors, but the blue pants had faded to purple. The orange retained its color. Consequently, that's how Clemson University derived its nickname (Tigers), mascot (the Tiger), and school colors (orange and purple).

SCHOOL NAME: Coastal Carolina University
NICKNAME: Chanticleers
MASCOT: rooster ("Chauncey")
COLORS: teal, bronze, and black
CONFERENCE: Sun Belt Conference

HISTORY

The official nickname and mascot for Coastal Carolina University's (CCU) athletic teams is the Chanticleer. When Coastal first started competing in college athletics in 1963, there was no athletic department, and when the university formed a basketball team, Cal F. Maddox, an English teacher, was asked to be the coach. CCU's original nickname and mascot was the Trojans, but Maddox proposed changing the name and mascot to the Chanticleers to several students. The chanticleer was a proud and fierce rooster that dominated the barnyard in one of Geoffrey Chaucer's Canterbury Tales, *The Nun's Priest Tale.* For Maddox's players to compete against seasoned teams, they would have to rely on something other than physical strength. Chaucer's rooster was saved from the hungry fox by his quick wit, plus the aid of Pertelote, the hen, and an old farm woman. Hence, Coastal players would have to use their heads and support one another as a team. The students agreed with Maddox and convinced the university to change the nickname and mascot to the Chanticleer.

When CCU was a part of the University of South Carolina (USC) school system, like USC, their school colors were garnet and black. When CCU became an independent public university in 1993, CCU's first president, Dr. Ronald Ingle, felt it was time for the university to have its own individual colors. He once saw his wife wearing a scarf that displayed the colors teal, bronze, and black. He liked this combination and decided to make them CCU's official school colors in 1994.

SCHOOL NAME: Colorado State University
NICKNAME: Rams
MASCOT: ram
COLORS: green and gold
CONFERENCE: Mountain West Conference

HISTORY

In 1944, Colorado State University (CSU) was called Colorado Agricultural and Mechanical Arts College, and its athletic teams were called the Aggies. When the school's name was changed to CSU in 1957, the official nickname was changed to the Rams in 1959. That name was chosen because the bighorn ram is indigenous to the state of Colorado's Rocky Mountains.

During the early days of CSU's football program, the college was called the Colorado Agricultural College, and the thought of having a college mascot was never discussed. But in 1912, when a dog showed up on campus, the idea of having a mascot came to life. During that time, the athletic teams were still called the Aggies, but the school's unofficial mascot became an English bulldog named Peanuts. Peanuts was purchased by a student named Floyd Cross and would often be seen roaming around the campus. Peanuts became quite popular, and students would often feed him peanuts as a snack. Unfortunately, in either April or May 1918, Peanuts was found dead after being poisoned by students from the University of Colorado. The bighorn ram was adopted as CSU's official mascot in 1959.

Since CSU was once a major college for agriculture, the school chose forest green and Vegas gold as its official school colors. The color green represents alfalfa, squash, and other crops, while gold represents golden wheat.

SCHOOL NAME:	Duke University
NICKNAME:	Blue Devils
MASCOT:	blue devil
COLORS:	blue and white
CONFERENCE:	Atlantic Coast Conference

HISTORY

When World War I ended in Europe in 1920, the Board of Trustees at Trinity College (now Duke University) lifted their twenty-five-year ban on intercollegiate athletic competition. In 1921, the school's newspaper, which was called the *Trinity Chronicle*, launched a campaign to select a new school name and mascot. To help raise enthusiasm regarding the selection process, a school pep rally was organized with the sole purpose of informing Trinity students that other competing colleges such as Georgia Tech and in-state rival North Carolina State were gaining national recognition as the Golden Tornados and the Wolf Pack. Because Trinity College was a Methodist school, students realized the school's current nicknames: the Trinity Eleven, Blue and White, and Methodist, were in dire need of a change. Believing that the colors dark blue and white (for the Methodist religion) would be appropriate, the newspaper editors presented these options for the mascot: Blue Titans, Blue Eagles, Polar Bears, Blue Devils, Royal Blazes, or Blue Warriors. In the end, no other nomination won strong favor but Blue Devils. This was probably due to the Chasseurs Alpines and Blue Devils gaining national recognition in 1915, when they toured the country in an effort to raise money after the United States entered WWI. The Blue Devils were well-known French soldiers who were infamous for their trench warfare tactics in their native region of the French Alps. Their distinctive blue uniforms, capes, and berets captured public imagination. But despite the strong acceptance of the Blue Devil name by students, it was not used because there was fear that opposition would arise on the Methodist campus from others that criticized the name for obvious reasons.

In 1922, the officers of the senior class agreed that in making final preparations for their final year, one of their goals should be to finally determine a school nickname and mascot from the 1920 selected nominations. The editors from Trinity College's other two school newspapers (the *Archive* and the *Chanticleer*) agreed that their staff should make the selection. When William H. Lander, editor-in-chief, and Mike Bradshaw, managing editor, for the *Trinity Chronicle*, started referring to the athletic teams as the Blue Devils during the 1922–23 season, the name caught on and was an instant success, with no criticism or opposition: not even from the college administration. The staff continued to use the name, so it eventually became the official nickname and mascot for Trinity College. In 1924, Trinity College changed its name to Duke University, in honor of Washington Duke, who was a big financial contributor to Trinity College. But the now new Duke University continued to use the name Blue Devil to represent the school's athletic teams and mascot.

SCHOOL NAME:	East Carolina University
NICKNAME:	Pirates
MASCOT:	pirate ("the Pirate")
COLORS:	purple and gold
CONFERENCE:	American Athletic Conference

HISTORY

In 1983, the Pirates became the official nickname for East Carolina University (ECU) sports teams for one main reason. Years ago, during the colonial days, pirates sided along the Pee Dee River, which flows through North and South Carolina.

Now that ECU had an official nickname, it was time to pick a mascot and decide on a name for that mascot. So the university decided to have a Name the Pirate contest that involved elementary schoolkids throughout Pitt County. The name PeeDee the Pirate was chosen and likely derived from the name of the river. PeeDee the Pirate, the costumed mascot, was then created in 1983. In 1985, ECU's chancellor decided that PeeDee the Pirate was not an appropriate name and renamed the mascot the Pirate. The student body was not happy about that because they were not involved in selecting a new name. To this day, many fans still refer to ECU's mascot as PeeDee the Pirate.

In 1909, when ECU students first arrived on campus, the administration asked the student body to vote on selecting school colors. The colors royal purple and old gold were chosen. Dr. Mary Jo Bratton, who was a historian at ECU and the author of *East Carolina University: The Formative Years 1907–1982,* said the selection of ECU's school colors by the student body was one of the school's first traditions.

SCHOOL NAME:	Eastern Michigan University
NICKNAME:	Eagles
MASCOT:	eagle ("Swoop")
COLORS:	green and white
CONFERENCE:	Mid-American Conference

HISTORY

Prior to Eastern Michigan University (EMU) changing its nickname to the Eagles in 1991, all of its sports teams were called the Hurons. On October 31, 1929, that name was chosen by a three-person committee (Dr. Clyde Ford, Dr. Elmer Lyman, and Prof. Bert Peet) who was responsible for running a contest to select the school nickname. The person who was responsible for coming up with the Huron nickname was George Hanner. George chose this name because, at that time, he worked at the Huron Hilton Hotel. He was deeply influenced by not only his employer's name but also the Huron Indian tribe that was well-known throughout Michigan and Ohio and migrated after leaving Quebec, Canada. In 1988, the Michigan Department of Human Rights issued a report suggesting that all schools that use Native American nicknames, mascots, or logos to promote their athletic teams discontinue doing so because they promote racial stereotypes. So a committee was formed to come up with a new school nickname. Three recommendations were made to the EMU Board of Regents, and on May 22, 1991, the name Eagles was chosen. The other two names that made the final list of recommendations were the Green Hornets and the Express.

After EMU changed its nickname to the Eagles in 1991, Swoop became the school's official mascot in 1994. Swoop is a costumed mascot depicted as an American bald eagle that wears an EMU jersey.

The official school colors for EMU's athletic teams are green and white. Unfortunately, there is no historical data explaining why those colors were chosen.

SCHOOL NAME:	Florida Atlantic University
NICKNAME:	Owls
MASCOT:	owl ("Owlsley the Owl")
COLORS:	blue, red, and silver
CONFERENCE:	Conference USA

HISTORY

When Florida Atlantic University (FAU) began competing in intercollegiate athletics in the mid-1980s, the school chose Owls as its official nickname. That name was chosen because the land that makes up FAU's campus was home to the burrowing owl long before FAU's inception in 1964. The owl also signifies wisdom, determination, and cognizance. In 1971, the National Audubon Society officially designated FAU's campus an owl sanctuary.

Owlsley the Owl, the official mascot for FAU athletic teams, is a costumed owl that can be seen at FAU sporting events.

Sometime after FAU's inception, a discussion took place between Adelaide Snyder, who was FAU's vice president of University Relations; Roger Miller, who was the top administrator officer; and other committee members to determine FAU's official school colors. Mr. Snyder suggested blue and tan, because blue would represent the sea and tan would represent the sand. Mr. Miller, who had just retired as a JAG colonel in the army, suggested that silver gray replace the tan because now that Mr. Miller was retired, he would never want to see the color tan again. Consequently, Mr. Snyder and the other committee members approved the color change. Over the years, red eventually became the third color. Today, blue and red are considered to be FAU's official colors, and silver gray is used as an accent.

SCHOOL NAME:	Florida International University
NICKNAME:	Panthers
MASCOT:	panther ("Roary the Panther")
COLORS:	blue and gold
CONFERENCE:	Conference USA

HISTORY

Prior to 1987, the nickname for Florida International University (FIU) athletic teams was the Panthers. That name was chosen because of the Florida panther being an endangered species to the nearby Everglades. FIU's original nickname was the Sunblazers and was changed to the Golden Panthers in 1987. The nickname was eventually shortened to the Panthers at the beginning of the 2010–11 school year.

Roary the Panther is the costumed mascot for FIU athletic teams and has been cheering along with FIU fans since 1987.

The school colors of FIU's athletic teams are blue and gold. One theory that might explain why those colors were chosen is that FIU's original nickname was the Sunblazers, which was represented by a giant sun as the mascot. Therefore, blue would represent the sky, and gold the sun. Consequently, even though FIU's nickname is now the Panthers, the panther is also gold, so the color scheme is still applicable.

SCHOOL NAME:	Florida State University
NICKNAME:	Seminoles
MASCOT:	seminal indian ("Chief Osceola")
COLORS:	garnet and gold
CONFERENCE:	Atlantic Coast Conference

HISTORY

The Seminole Indians were one of the, if not the first group of, settlers to live in the state of Florida. Long known for their strong sense of determination, nobility, bravery, and courage, Florida State University (FSU) selected them to represent the school's nickname and mascot.

In 1904 and 1905, Florida State University's (formally Florida State College) football teams won championships wearing the colors purple and gold. In 1905, Florida State College became an all-girl school. As a result, the football team was forced to relocate to an all-male school in Tallahassee. That same year, the student body at the new Florida State College for Women (FSCW) elected to use crimson as the school's official color and then later decided to combine the colors purple and crimson, which resulted in the color of garnet. In 1947, FSCW became a coeducational college and changed its name to Florida State University. This was also the same year that the FSU football team wore their now famous garnet and gold color uniforms: they played and lost 14–6 to Stetson University.

SCHOOL NAME:	Fresno State University
NICKNAME:	Bulldogs
MASCOT:	bulldog
COLORS:	cardinal and blue
CONFERENCE:	Mountain West Conference

HISTORY

In the fall of 1921, student body president Warren Moody and his friends became part of a very odd but historical event. Almost every day, they found themselves greeted by a white bulldog outside the main campus building. In time, the group grew so attached to the dog that they got the idea to make the bulldog the school mascot. When Arids Walker made the motion in a student body meeting, the motion was accepted. As a result, on November 21, 1921, the Bulldogs were adopted as the official school nickname and mascot for Fresno State University.

Fresno State University formed when Fresno Normal School and Fresno Junior College decided to combine their institutions to create one major university. When the time came to select an official school color for the newly formed Fresno State University, the women from the old normal school wanted blue and white, while the men from the now defunct junior college wanted red and white. In the end, both parties came to a compromise and chose red and blue. Eventually, red changed to cardinal.

SCHOOL NAME:	Georgia Institute of Technology
NICKNAME:	Yellow Jackets
MASCOT:	yellow jacket bee ("Buzz") and "Ramblin Wreck"
COLORS:	old gold and white
CONFERENCE:	Atlantic Coast Conference

HISTORY

When the Georgia Institute of Technology (GT) was first established, its athletic teams were known as the Golden Tornados. This name was likely chosen because of the first two letters of the school's name being GT. As an expression of team spirit and support, it soon became a fad for tech students to wear yellow jackets to sporting events. In time, the name Yellow Jackets, associated with the yellow jacket bee, became the school's new nickname and mascot. However, the school's first official mascot was actually a 1930 Ford Model A Sports Coupe called the Ramblin Wreck. Since 1961, the Wreck has led GT's football team onto the field at every home game. The color of the Wreck is gold and white and has two gold flags that read "To Hell with Georgia" and "Give 'Em Hell Tech."

The official school colors for GT's athletic teams are old gold and white. Unfortunately, there is no historical data explaining why those colors were chosen.

SCHOOL NAME: Georgia Southern University
NICKNAME: Eagles
MASCOT: eagle ("Freedom" and "Gus")
COLORS: blue and white
CONFERENCE: Sun Belt Conference

HISTORY

The official nickname and mascot for Georgia Southern University (GSU) athletic teams is the Eagles. In 1959, that name was chosen by a very close student vote instead of the Colonels, after the school was renamed Georgia State College. From 1924 to 1941, they were called the Blue Tide, and after WWII, they were referred to as the Professors because of the school being a teachers college at the time.

The official mascot for GSU athletic teams is a male Southern bald eagle named Freedom. Freedom was first discovered in Maitland, Florida, in 2004, after being knocked out of his nest. He injured his beak and got an infection. After being taken to the Florida Audubon Center for Birds of Prey, Freedom made a full recovery. However, the injury to his beak was permanent and prevented Freedom from returning to the wild. After getting permission from the United States Fish and Wildlife Services, GSU acquired him as their mascot. GSU also has a costumed eagle mascot named Gus.

The official school colors for GSU athletic teams are blue and white. Those colors were chosen because in 1982, when GSU revived their football team, the school did not have a lot of money to purchase fancy uniforms, so the team wore plain white pants and blue jerseys without their names on the back. Consequently, Coach Erik Russell ordered solid blue helmets and asked his players to put a white strip of tape down the middle. Following the success of the Eagles, GSU decided to continue to use the same basic design and colors for their teams.

SCHOOL NAME: Georgia State University
NICKNAME: Panthers
MASCOT: panther ("Pounce")
COLORS: blue and white
CONFERENCE: Sun Belt Conference

HISTORY

In 1955, Panthers was chosen as the official nickname for Georgia State University (GSU) athletic teams by the student body.

From 1940 to 1946, GSU was a night school called the Georgia Evening School with an owl as the mascot. Then in 1947, for an unknown reason, the nickname was changed to the Ramblers. In 1955, the nickname was changed once again by the student body to the Panthers. However, the school did not yet have an official mascot. Therefore, in 1980, Claws, a costumed blue panther, made his debut to support the school's basketball team. In 1989, he was replaced by Urbie, who was a crimson costumed panther. Finally, in 1993, Pounce, a cartoonish muscular blue panther, became GSU's official mascot.

The official school colors for GSU's athletic teams are blue and white. Unfortunately, there is no historical data explaining why those colors were chosen.

SCHOOL NAME:	Indiana University
NICKNAME:	Hoosiers
MASCOT:	hoosier
COLORS:	cream and crimson
CONFERENCE:	Big Ten Conference

HISTORY

When discussing college nicknames, one question that always seems to surface as a hot topic is, "What is a Hoosier?" Or, "Why are the Indiana University (IU) athletic teams called the Hoosiers?" Well, the answer is quite unique.

Prior to becoming a state in 1816, Indiana was a part of North America's Northwest Territory. The first people to settle in this area in 1679 were known as Hoosiers, for their unusual saying when greeting strangers, "Who's yere?" After becoming a state, Indiana became known as the Hoosier state. For this reason, the name Hoosier was selected as IU's official nickname and chosen to be the university's mascot.

When IU finally decided that it was time for the university to select an official school color, cream and crimson were chosen by the class of 1888.

SCHOOL NAME: Iowa State University
NICKNAME: Cyclones
MASCOT: cardinal ("Cy")
COLORS: cardinal and gold
CONFERENCE: Big 12 Conference

HISTORY

Iowa State University (ISU) became known as the Cyclones in 1885, after a headline and sports article in the *Chicago Tribune* described how the ISU football team soundly defeated Northwestern University 36–0. It read, "Struck by a Cyclone. It comes from Iowa and devastates Evanston (home of Northwestern University)." Since then, all ISU athletic teams have been known as the Cyclones.

Even though ISU athletic teams have the nickname Cyclones, the university's mascot is a cardinal. The reason? Prior to ISU adopting the Cyclone nickname, they were formally called the Cardinals. Furthermore, since Chev Adams, who was the president of the Collegiate Manufacturing Company (a company that manufactures stuffed animals) in Ames, Iowa, said, "We cannot make a stuffed cyclone!" ISU students decided to stick with the cardinal after an on-campus mascot contest was held. The name Cy was given to the university mascot after Mrs. Ed Ohlsen, the wife of a faculty member, won the Name the Bird contest in 1954. Her reason for choosing the name Cy was very simple—it was short for Cyclone. Adams elected to donate a mascot costume to ISU as a result of the contest. So Cy made his first appearance at ISU's 1955 homecoming.

ISU did not always bear the colors cardinal and red either. The original school colors were gold, black, and silver, of which all three colors represented something different. Gold represented agriculture's golden harvest, black represented the school's veterinary department, and silver represented engineering. After the ISU Athletic Council found out that it would be impossible to use that color combination to dye the school sweaters, they decided to keep the color gold but replaced silver and black with the color cardinal. The reason? Cardinal represents ISU's original nickname.

SCHOOL NAME: Kansas State University
NICKNAME: Wildcat
MASCOT: wildcat ("Willie")
COLORS: royal purple
CONFERENCE: Big 12 Conference

HISTORY

The Wildcat has been Kansas State University's (K-State) nickname and mascot since 1920. The nickname was first used in 1915 by Coach John "Chief" Bender because of the football team's "fighting spirit." Prior to 1915, K-Staters were known as the Aggies because Aggies is short for "agriculture," which was a dominant field of study at K-State. Then in 1917, Coach Charles Bachman renamed it to the Farmers. Then the Wildcats nickname finally stuck when Coach Charles Bachman began using it again in 1920. The name was chosen because it symbolizes K-State sports. However, the mascot's name, Willie, was not used until the early 1960s, when a reporter used the name Willie the Wildcat in a story. That name stuck and became synonymous with K-State.

In 1896, senior class members Winnifred Houghton, Minnie L. Copeland Jr., and Ina E. Holyrod selected royal purple as K-State's official school colors. White and silver are used as complementary colors.

SCHOOL NAME:	Kent State University
NICKNAME:	Golden Flashes
MASCOT:	golden eagle ("Flash")
COLORS:	blue and gold
CONFERENCE:	Mid-American Conference

HISTORY

The athletic teams at Kent State University have not always been nicknamed the Golden Flashes. In fact, the story of how the university got its nickname has been a topic of debate. Legend has it that, originally, teams at Kent State were called the Silver Foxes. John E. McGilvrey, Kent State's president, takes credit for this because the name was originally based on his silver fox farm, which was located east of campus. After his dismissal in 1926, acting president T. Howard Winters organized a contest to select a new school nickname. The winner would receive twenty-five dollars. After Golden Flashes got approval from the student body and the faculty athletic committee, it became the new official nickname for Kent State University. The first athletic team to use the new name was the 1927 basketball team.

When the Kent State mascot selection committee realized that it would be very difficult to construct an animated lightning bolt (Golden Flashes) costume, they selected the golden eagle as the official mascot for the university. Their decision gave the university the option of having a live or costumed mascot.

The official school colors of Kent State University's athletic teams are blue and gold. Those colors were inspired by the university's first president, John McGilvrey. When he was a faculty member at the University of Illinois, McGilvrey liked the blue and orange color combinations, which were that school's colors. Consequently, the color combinations of blue and orange and blue and gold were interchangeably used by McGilvrey. The colors blue and gold were officially adopted as Kent State's colors in 1925 by a committee vote.

SCHOOL NAME: Liberty University
NICKNAME: Flames, Lady Flames
MASCOT: eagle ("Sparky")
COLORS: red, white, and blue
CONFERENCE: Division I FBS Independents

HISTORY

In 1956, Jerry Falwell, along with a congregation of thirty-five other people, established the Thomas Roads Baptist Church (TRBC) in Lynchburg, Virginia. In February 1971, he founded the Lynchburg Baptist College (LBC) and appointed Dr. Elmer Towns as the vice president and academic dean. That same year, Dr. Towns interviewed Mr. Falwell to discuss TRBC's rapid growth. At this interview, the two of them produced a top-selling book in the United States titled *Church Aflame.* As a result, LBC's motto became "Knowledge Aflame." That motto eventually led to Liberty University adopting the Flames and Lady Flames as the official nickname for the university's men's and women's athletic teams. LBC changed its name to Liberty University is 1985.

The official mascot for Liberty University's athletic teams is an eagle named Sparky. The idea for making an eagle the mascot came about when Dallas Cowboys head coach Tom Landry gave a speech at a prebanquet press conference for Lynchburg business leaders. At the banquet, Liberty Baptist College (formally Lynchburg Baptist College) introduced its 1980 theme, "Fly with the Flames." The theme displayed an eagle substituting the letter *F* in the word "flames."

When Lynchburg Baptist College changed its name to Liberty Baptist College during the 1975–76 school academic year, the college also changed its school colors from green and gold, to red, white, and blue. Those colors remained the same and continued to be the official colors for the school's athletic teams, even after the school changed its name to Liberty University in 1985.

SCHOOL NAME:	Louisiana State University
NICKNAME:	Tigers
MASCOT:	tiger ("Mike V")
COLORS:	purple and gold
CONFERENCE:	Southeastern Conference

HISTORY

The Civil War had a lot to do with Louisiana State University (LSU) selecting the tiger as its official mascot. Apparently, during the war, there were two Louisiana brigades in the Army of Northern Virginia who were heralded for their bravery and fierce fighting spirit. They became known as the Louisiana Tigers. In recognition of the two brigades, LSU officials elected to have a tiger represent the school's nickname, mascot, and athletic teams.

The name Mike V was given to LSU's Bengal tiger mascot in honor of Mike Chambers, who was the trainer for Sheik, LSU's first Bengal tiger mascot. The Roman numeral V represents the fifth Bengal tiger mascot to be associated with LSU.

Prior to LSU playing in its very first intercollegiate football game, the school's official colors were blue and white. In preparation for their showdown with state rival Tulane University, Coach Charles Coates and quarterback Ruffin Pleasant, along with other football players, went to New Orleans to buy blue and white ribbons to enhance school spirit. However, with Mardi Gras fast approaching, the store they visited only had purple and gold ribbons on hand. Coach Coates and company decided to buy the ribbons and use them as the school decorations. Needless to say, the new color combination went over big with LSU students and fans and was eventually adopted as LSU's new official school colors.

SCHOOL NAME:	Louisiana Tech University
NICKNAME:	Bulldogs
MASCOT:	english bulldog ("Tech")
COLORS:	red and blue
CONFERENCE:	Conference USA

HISTORY

The official nickname for all Louisiana Tech University (La. Tech) athletic teams is the Bulldogs. That name was chosen because, according to legend, in 1899, five La. Tech students adopted a bulldog that had been seen wandering around campus. Shortly after that, a fire broke out at their residence while they were asleep. The boys were able to escape the burning building after being awakened by the sound of the bulldog barking. Sadly, the dog was overcome by smoke inhalation and never made it out of the house. The students buried the dog on campus.

The mascot for La. Tech athletic teams, both past and present, is an English bulldog named Tech. Tech I was the original mascot that was donated to the university by the Mathews family in 1930. Since then, La. Tech has had twenty-one (I–XXII) Tech replacements. The mascot is owned by the Student Government Association (SGA) and resides with either a faculty member or a local alumnus selected by the SGA.

La. Tech's school colors are red and blue. Those colors were chosen back in 1896 by Colonel A. T. Prescott, who was the president of what was then called the Louisiana Polytechnic Institute. Prescott said that red and blue represent the courage and loyalty of the institution.

SCHOOL NAME:	Marshall University
NICKNAME:	Thundering Herd
MASCOT:	"Marco the Bison"
COLORS:	kelly green and white
CONFERENCE:	Conference USA

HISTORY

In 1910, Marshall University's nickname was the Big Green. This, of course, was in reference to the university's team uniforms. However, when *Huntington Herald-Dispatch* sportswriter Duke Ridgley referred to a late 1920s squad as a Thundering Herd, it caught on quickly. He got the idea from a movie based on the 1925 Zane Gray novel of the same name. Later that year, football coach Charles "Trusty" Tallman was able to give Marshall its first win of the season. As a result, newspaper headlines everywhere read, "Trusty Tallman's Thundering Herd." Consequently, both Thundering Herd and Big Green were used in reference to Marshall University.

In the fall of 1964, Stewart Smith, who was the president of Marshall University, felt that the name Big Green was too boring. So he decided to appoint a committee made up of both faculty and students to come up with one official school nickname. The committee narrowed its choices down to three names: Big Green, the Thundering Herd, and the Rams. On January 5, 1965, over 85 percent of the Marshall student body picked Thundering Herd above the others, chose the buffalo as the official mascot, and selected kelly green and white as the official school colors.

Marco the Bison is the official mascot of Marshall University. The name Marco was derived as a combination of the school's original name, which was Marshall College.

SCHOOL NAME: Miami University
NICKNAME: RedHawks
MASCOT: hawk
COLORS: red and white
CONFERENCE: Mid-American Conference

HISTORY

Miami University has not always had the RedHawk nickname. In fact, there were several Miami athletic team nicknames prior to the RedHawks selection in 1997.

Back in the 1930–31 school year, Ralph McGinnis, who was the editor of the Miami alumni magazine, announced that Redskins would replace Big Red as the school's official nickname. McGinnis felt that a change was needed since Denison University, which is also located in Ohio, shared the same name, which caused confusion. What's more, even after Miami changed its nickname, there was even more confusion among Miami students because *the Miami Student*, the university's newspaper, used the names Redskins and Big Red interchangeably. Prior to 1928, Miami athletic teams were referred to as the Miami Boys, the Big Red Ones, and the Red and Whites.

In the 1990s, Miami University officials were urged to change the Redskins nickname because many, if not all American Indians, found the name to be offensive and discriminatory. Moreover, when an Oklahoma-based Miami tribe also urged the university to change its name, the Miami Board of Trustees voted to discontinue the Redskins nickname on September 26, 1996. On April 19, 1997, the board voted to adopt the nickname RedHawks.

Since all Miami University athletic teams were once referred to as the Big Reds and the Big Reds and Whites, university officials chose the color combination of red and white as the official colors for Miami University.

SCHOOL NAME:	Michigan State University
NICKNAME:	Spartans
MASCOT:	spartan ("Sparty")
COLORS:	green and white
CONFERENCE:	Big Ten Conference

HISTORY

In 1925, Michigan Agricultural College changed its name to Michigan State College. Consequently, the college organized a contest to select a new nickname. As a result, the name Aggies was replaced with the Michigan Staters. George S. Alderton, a sports editor for the *Lansing State Journal*, complained that the new nickname was very unmanageable when writing sports articles, so he was determined to find a better one. After contacting a friend who worked in Michigan State's Information Services Department, Mr. Alderton was able to get a hold of the entry listings left over from the school's contest. In doing so, he came across the name Spartans and was convinced that this was the name that he had been searching for. Unfortunately, he forgot to write down the name of the person who submitted the entry. To this day, the person responsible for this great achievement remains a mystery. After taking it upon himself to use the nickname Spartan in his sports articles, the new name was an instant hit with students, faculty, and fans alike. Hence, Spartans became the new official nickname and, in time, the mascot (Sparty) for Michigan State University.

Although the details are sketchy, records from Michigan Agricultural College's Athletic Association show that on April 11, 1899, the colors green and white were first used on the school's monogram, which was worn by students competing in intercollegiate events.

SCHOOL NAME: Middle Tennessee State University
NICKNAME: Blue Raiders
MASCOT: winged horse ("Lightning")
COLORS: blue and white
CONFERENCE: Conference USA

HISTORY

The official nickname for Middle Tennessee State University (MT) athletic teams is the Blue Raiders. In 1934, that name was chosen from a contest organized by the *Daily News Journal*. The person that came up with the winning nickname was Chris Sarver, who was an MT football player.

MT's original mascot was Nathen Bedford Forest, who was a Confederate general and early leader in the Ku Klux Klan. Because of Forest being associated with the Klan, in 1970, MT decided to change its mascot to a blue-colored scent hound dog named Old Blue. Prior to MT's football team upgrading to Division I-A status in 1999, in 1998, it once again changed its mascot to a blue-winged horse named Lightning. The name Lightning symbolizes MT's aerospace program, and the horse symbolizes MT's horse science program and the region's heritage in the walking horse industry.

The official school colors of MT's athletic teams are blue and white. Unfortunately, there is no historical data explaining why those colors were chosen.

SCHOOL NAME:	Mississippi State University
NICKNAME:	Bulldogs
MASCOT:	english bulldog ("Bully")
COLORS:	maroon and white
CONFERENCE:	Southeastern Conference

HISTORY

The official nickname of all athletic teams at Mississippi State University is the Bulldogs. However, years ago, when the university was called Mississippi A&M College, the teams were referred to as the Aggies, which is short for "agriculture." This was due to Mississippi A&M being an agricultural college. Then when the school changed its name to Mississippi State College in 1932, the teams became the Maroons. This was a result of the school nickname being synonymous with the team uniforms. Then in 1961, not long after the school became known as Mississippi State University, Bulldogs were chosen as the official nickname. This name was chosen because of the tough and tenacious play that had been displayed by the teams over the years.

The official mascot of Mississippi State University is Bully, an English bulldog.

When Mississippi A&M College first established a football team in 1895, the school's student body eagerly requested that the team choose its uniform colors prior to their first intercollegiate football game against Southern Baptist University (now called Union University) on November 15. As a gesture of honor, the football team decided to leave the color selection up to W. M. Matthews, the team captain. In doing so, he chose, without hesitation, maroon and white. From that point on, maroon and white had become the official school colors for Mississippi State University.

SCHOOL NAME:	New Mexico State University
NICKNAME:	Aggies
MASCOT:	gunslinger ("Pistol Pete")
COLORS:	crimson and white
CONFERENCE:	Division I FBS Independents

HISTORY

Back in the early 1800s, people known as settlers traveled to the western part of the country in search of a better life to make their home. The settlers that lived in the southwestern region were faced with the challenge of trying to grow food in the desert. In time, they learned, thus mastering the art of agriculture. As an institution known for its agricultural department, New Mexico State University (NMSU) chose Aggies (short for "agriculture") as their official nickname.

Pistol Pete was chosen as the official mascot for NMSU athletic teams for a good reason. He was a real-life Western gunslinger! His real name was Frank Eaton, and as a child, his father was killed by six brothers from two different families, the Campseys (four brothers) and the Ferbers (two brothers). All of them were regulators. By age fifteen, Frank was a quick draw and a marksman but decided to go to the Fort Gibson cavalry in the northeast part of the Indian Territory to improve his skills. It was there where Frank got the name Pistol Pete. In Albuquerque, in 1881, Pistol Peter killed those six brothers in a gunfight.

Crimson and white are the official school colors for NMSU athletic teams. Crimson represents power, vigor, strength, and leadership. As an agricultural institution, NMSU chose white because it symbolizes spring and summer, the two seasons when crops are planted.

SCHOOL NAME: North Carolina State University
NICKNAME: Wolfpack
MASCOT: wolf (Mr. and Ms. "Wuf" and "Tuffy")
COLORS: red and white
CONFERENCE: Atlantic Coast Conference

HISTORY

During the early years when North Carolina State University (NC State) started taking an active role in intercollegiate athletics, the school's teams were often referred to as the Farmers, Mechanics, Aggies, the Techs, and Red Terrors. However, when discussing the idea behind what is now the official nickname of NC State athletic teams, there are two separate stories that explain how the Wolfpack name was derived. The first story states that sometime in 1921, the name was brought about by a disgruntled fan who told athletic officials that the football team would never have a winning season as long as the players behaved "like a wolf pack." The second story explains that prior to the September 24, 1921, football game against Randolph Macon, head football Coach Harry Hartsell, who replaced Coach Fetzer, was responsible for adopting the name. Initially, students laughed at this description but later started referring to NC State football teams as the Wolfpack. For the next twenty years, Wolfpack became the common household name. With negative connotations associated with the name Wolfpack (nickname for World War II Nazi submarines), NC State school chancellor J. W. Harrelson organized a school contest to determine an official nickname for all the NC State athletic teams. When all the votes were in, the student majority still selected Wolfpack as the new name. Harrelson accepted defeat gracefully, and in 1947, university officials decided that all NC State athletic teams would be called the Wolfpack.

The official mascots for NC State athletic teams are Mr. and Ms. Wuf, which are costumed animals and a live dog (Tuffy), which is supposed to impersonate Tuffy, NC State's cartoon strutting wolf. In the past, NC State used live wolves, but for some reason, people thought it was too dangerous.

Although red and white are the official colors of North Carolina State University's athletic teams, those colors weren't adopted until 1896. From 1892 to 1894, the school colors were pink and blue. Then in 1895, students wanted a different color, so they chose brown and white. In 1896, students wanted another change, and the overwhelming chose red and white. The board of trustees would only agree to the students' new color selection if they promised to never ask for another color change again. Hence, red and white have been NC State's colors ever since.

SCHOOL NAME: Northern Illinois University
NICKNAME: Huskies
MASCOT: husky ("Victor E. Huskie")
COLORS: cardinal and black
CONFERENCE: Mid-American Conference

HISTORY

From 1899 to 1939, Northern Illinois University (NIU) athletic teams went through a series of nicknames. Those names included the Profs, Cardinals, and Evansmen. Evansmen was chosen in honor of George Evans, who was NIU's head football and basketball coach from 1929 to 1954. In 1940, Huskies was chosen as the official nickname.

NIU's mascot was also chosen in 1940 by a four-man committee whose names were George Evans, Harold Taxman, Walter Lorimer, and Harry Telman. All of them were members of NIU's Varsity Club. After much debate, a Siberian husky was chosen as the official mascot. NIU's current mascot is a costumed husky named Victor E. Huskie.

NIU, which was originally named Northern Illinois State Normal School (NISNS), adopted yellow and white as their school colors. Those colors were chosen by a committee in 1899. The head of the committee was Emma F. Stratford. In 1906, NISNS decided to go with cardinal and black because yellow and white became distorted on the football team's uniforms when they got dirty. When NISNS became NIU, the school decided to keep cardinal and black as the official school colors of their athletic teams.

SCHOOL NAME:	Northwestern University
NICKNAME:	Wildcats
MASCOT:	wildcat ("Willie")
COLORS:	purple and white
CONFERENCE:	Big Ten Conference

HISTORY

Northwestern University (NU) adopted Wildcats as their official school nickname after Wallace Abbey, a sportswriter for the *Chicago Tribune*, used a catchy phrase when describing the Northwestern versus Chicago football game played in 1924. With neither team being able to score any points for fifty-seven minutes, Abbey described how NU stopped Chicago from scoring from their own nine-yard line by saying, ". . . once they had the ball on the 9 yard line and had been stopped dead by a purple wall of wildcats." From that time on, all of Northwestern's athletic teams were called the Wildcats.

Nine years after NU selected Wildcats as their official nickname, the NU athletic department teamed up with an advertising agency and created the caricature Willie. In 1947, the mascot Willie the Wildcat came to life when four students from the Alpha Delta fraternity dressed up in wildcat costumes for NU's homecoming float.

When NU's faculty realized just how much school spirit could be achieved from a college athletic team bearing its own official colors, a committee was formed in 1894 to make a determination. As a result, the colors purple and white were selected, not only for the athletic teams but also for the entire university.

SCHOOL NAME:	Ohio State University
NICKNAME:	Buckeyes
MASCOT:	buckeye ("Brutus")
COLORS:	scarlet and gray
CONFERENCE:	Big Ten Conference

HISTORY

Native Ohioans are known as Buckeyes, which is a tree that grows quite abundantly throughout the state of Ohio. To add, this infamous nickname was also passed down to Ohio State University (OSU) students, athletes, and alumni. Because the buckeye tree (related to the horse chestnut tree) has a mahogany-colored seed attached to its leaves that is the size of an olive, it has been a long-standing tradition to place buckeye leaves on the helmets of OSU football players as a reward for outstanding performances.

With the buckeye tree having such an impact on the state of Ohio and OSU alike, it only seemed obvious to have a buckeye represent OSU as the university's official mascot as well. The selection committee unanimously came to that decision, and Brutus was the name eventually given to OSU's biggest fan.

In 1878, the OSU selection committee chose orange and black as the school's official colors. However, when they learned that Princeton University had already chosen that color combination, the committee switched to scarlet and gray.

SCHOOL NAME: Ohio University
NICKNAME: Bobcats
MASCOT: bobcat ("Mr. Bobcat")
COLORS: olive green and white
CONFERENCE: Mid-American Conference

HISTORY

In the early days of college athletics, the teams at Ohio University (OU) were simply known as the Nameless Wonders. Needless to say, the OU athletic board agreed that it was now time for a school nickname. In 1925, the OU athletic board decided to hold a contest to select a nickname that would represent all the school's athletic teams. The winner would receive a prize of ten dollars. After much discussion, Hal H. Roland, who was a former OU student and a resident of Athens, Ohio (home of OU), was awarded the ten dollars for his Bobcat entry. The first athletic team to try out the new name was the 1925–26 basketball team. The Bobcat nickname was an obvious success because OU defeated Denison University 33–21.

Now that OU had a nickname, the school decided it was now time for a mascot. In 1960, the men of Lincoln Hall agreed that instead of entering a float into the school's annual homecoming competition, they would create something that would be more memorable. As a result, Tom Schants created a large papier-mâché bobcat head that had a green hand-knitted sweater with "Ohio" written across the front in white letters. Because the costume was not designed to accommodate any person over five feet eleven inches, Lincoln Hall resident Dan Nichols was chosen to wear the suit. He was immediately hailed by OU students and fans alike as a good luck symbol when OU defeated archrival Miami University for the first time in fourteen years. In doing so, OU ended the season undefeated and was named NCAA champions.

Blue and white were the first colors chosen to represent OU athletic teams. However, in time, these colors created a lot of confusion in pennants, decorations, and so forth. OU's number-one archrival at that time was Marietta College, whose colors were also blue and white. As a result, during the summer of 1896, the question of suitable school colors was brought to the attention of Charles G. O'Bleness, who at that time was the manager of the OU football team. When trying to determine a new color, Mr. O'Bleness decided to consult with longtime friend Samuel Macmillen, who was the coach of Dartmouth College and resided in Springfield, Ohio, during the summer. When the color question was raised to Mr. Macmillen, he suggested olive green and white, Dartmouth's colors. Moreover, at his request, Mr. Macmillen sent Mr. O'Bleness his own Dartmouth sweater by express mail so that he could sample the colors. Delighted by what he saw, Mr. O'Bleness presented the sweater to the OU faculty and student body for approval at the college chapel. After various comments and expressions by all in attendance, Mr. Clyde Brown, a faculty member, asked Mr. O'Bleness to put on the sweater so that he could see how it would look. Then Mr. O'Bleness put the motion of the colors to a vote. It was unanimous, and olive green and white became the official school colors of OU.

SCHOOL NAME:	Oklahoma State University
NICKNAME:	Cowboys
MASCOT:	cowboy ("Pistol Pete")
COLORS:	orange and black
CONFERENCE:	Big 12 Conference

HISTORY

Around 1923, Oklahoma State A&M College (now Oklahoma State University) was in search of a new school mascot to replace their old one, which was a tiger. One day, a group of Oklahoma State University (OSU) students decided to attend the Armistice Day Parade, which was an annual event held near OSU. While there, they saw Frank "Pistol Pete" Eaton leading the event and decided to ask him if he would be interested in becoming OSU's new mascot. To their excitement, he said yes. You see, Pistol Pete was a local legend. He was an Oklahoma-born cowboy whose fascinating and exciting life experiences had captured both local and national attention. Upon accepting his new social role as the official OSU mascot, the likeness of Pistol Pete was immediately captured in T-shirts, stickers, and other OSU products that signified OSU's new nickname and mascot. To date, Pistol Pete is still one of the more recognizable college mascots seen at athletic events.

Before OSU adopted the cowboy as the school's official nickname and mascot, they used to be called the Tigers. The idea of using a tiger and the orange-and-black color combination was copied from Princeton University. When OSU changed its mascot to a cowboy, school officials decided to stay with the orange and black colors.

SCHOOL NAME:	Old Dominion University
NICKNAME:	Monarchs
MASCOT:	lion ("Big Blue")
COLORS:	blue and silver
CONFERENCE:	Conference USA

HISTORY

Before Old Dominion University (ODU) became ODU, it was the Norfolk Division of the College of William and Mary. Before surpassing the College of William and Mary's enrollment numbers and achieving its own four-year status, its athletic teams were known as the Braves, which was a derivation of William and Mary's nickname, the Indians. As a four-year university, ODU decided to change its nickname to the Monarchs. This name was chosen because the College of William and Mary's name originates from the Virginia colony founded by King Charles II, after the state pledged its loyalty to the crown during the English Civil War. Moreover, in addition to William III and Mary II making this large investment that resulted in the school being founded in 1693, they also ruled England at the invitation of Parliament as "joint monarchs."

The mascot for ODU athletic teams is a lion named Big Blue. A lion was chosen because it represents the king of the monarchs.

When ODU was known as the Norfolk Division of the College of William and Mary in 1930, the school colors were green and gold. Those colors were chosen out of respect for its parent institution, the College of William and Mary. As a way to distinguish itself from William and Mary, the division added the color gray. When ODU became an independent institution in 1962, the colors were changed to blue and white. In 1986, Joseph M. Marchello, ODU's new president, decided to change the colors to blue and silver as part of a new branding campaign, which included a lion with a crown. Marchello made this change after observing the presence of a newfound school sprit among students, faculty, and staff. The change also included updating the school mascot to Big Blue.

SCHOOL NAME:	Oregon State University
NICKNAME:	Beavers
MASCOT:	beaver ("Benny Beaver")
COLORS:	orange and black
CONFERENCE:	Pacific 12 Conference

HISTORY

Initially, when Oregon State University (OSU) athletic teams wore drab gray-and-tan sweatshirt jerseys, they were referred to as the Aggies. When the athletic teams started wearing orange jerseys, the nickname became the Orangemen. When OSU's school yearbook changed its name to the Beaver in 1916, the name Beaver became associated with the school. As a result, because the beaver is the state animal for Oregon, it only seemed appropriate for OSU to officially make that the nickname for all of its athletic teams.

Sometime after OSU football team started competing in college athletics, their mascot was a coyote named Jimmie. Then in 1909, the football team elected to change its mascot to a replica of Dr. John Bell (Doc Bell), who was a pastor and native of Corvallis (the location of OSU). The football team chose Dr. Bell as their mascot because of his steadfast attendance and advising. In an attempt to energize OSU's student body because of lagging school spirit, OSU's rally squad introduced Benny Beaver to OSU fans on September 18, 1952. Benny Beaver was well accepted by his fans and became OSU's official mascot.

Until the mid-1890s, OSU was called Corvallis College, and the school color was navy blue. John Bloss, who was the school's president, decided to form a faculty committee to vote on a new color. The committee chose the color orange. During that same period, a local tailor named J. H. Harris donated black uniforms to the baseball team. Legend has it that this is why OSU decided to make orange and black their official school colors.

SCHOOL NAME: Pennsylvania State University
NICKNAME: Nittany Lions
MASCOT: nittany lion
COLORS: blue and white
CONFERENCE: Big Ten Conference

HISTORY

In 1906, Pennsylvania State University (Penn State) selected Nittany Lions as the university's official nickname and mascot. The person responsible for this achievement was a student by the name of Joe Mason. He got the idea after seeing the Princeton University tiger mascot while traveling with the Penn State baseball team to New Jersey. As a result, Penn State is believed to be the first university to use a lion as a mascot.

The mountain lion, or Nittany Lion, was chosen because this animal once lived and roamed the mountains in central Pennsylvania. Furthermore, since Penn State is located in the Nittany Valley at the foot of Mount Nittany, the lion was designated the name Nittany Lion.

Penn State's school colors were not always blue and white. In October 1887, a three-member student committee was formed to select an official color combination for the university and its athletic teams. Dark pink and black were the colors unanimously selected. However, after several weeks of exposure to the sun, the uniforms faded to white. At that point, the committee decided to replace black with blue. So on March 18, 1890, blue and white were selected to represent Penn State.

SCHOOL NAME:	Purdue University
NICKNAME:	Boilermakers
MASCOT:	boilermaker ("Purdue Pete")
COLORS:	old gold and black
CONFERENCE:	Big 10 Conference

HISTORY

Years ago, it was not a requirement for colleges competing in intercollegiate athletics to have their athletes attend college. This was true for Purdue University's 1891 athletic teams, which were partially composed of factory workers that the Purdue athletic department recruited from a local boiler manufacturing company. When Purdue's team beat nearby school rival Wabash College 44–0, Wabash students took an immediate disliking to anyone associated with Purdue University, mainly their athletes. To help reinforce this attitude, many Wabash students tried to discredit Purdue (a highly respected engineering and agricultural school) and its students by saying that the university was made up of nothing more than a bunch of engineers, farmers, and boilermakers. However, in doing so, Wabash students found out to their surprise that the Purdue students took an instant liking to the name Boilermakers. So much so in fact that the school decided to use the name to represent Purdue University's official nickname and mascot. In time, they also selected Purdue Pete as the name for the university mascot.

The year 1887 was the first time Purdue University had an intercollegiate football team. To help honor that achievement, many of the football players felt that the team should be distinguished by certain colors. At that time, Princeton University was nationally recognized for its football success. Their colors were orange and black, although most people thought their colors were yellow and black. Purdue's football team chose black but opted to go with old gold instead of yellow. From that time on, Purdue athletic teams have been flying those colors, which is still endured today.

SCHOOL NAME: Rice University

NICKNAME: Owls

MASCOT: owl

COLORS: blue and gray

CONFERENCE: Conference USA

HISTORY

When Rice Institute (now Rice University) first started competing in intercollegiate athletics in 1912, the school chose the owl of Athena as its official nickname and mascot because of it being the symbol of wisdom. The year 1912 was also the year that Edger Odell Lovett, Rice University's president, chose blue and gray as the school's official colors.

SCHOOL NAME:	Rutgers University
NICKNAME:	Scarlet Knights
MASCOT:	scarlet knight
COLORS:	scarlet and black
CONFERENCE:	Big Ten Conference

HISTORY

Years ago, Rutgers University (RU) was called Queen's College. It was not until 1825 that the name was changed to Rutgers University in honor of Col. Henry Rutgers, a former school trustee and Revolutionary War veteran. In 1925 and for the next thirty years, the school's mascot was a chanticleer, and its nickname was the Queensmen. In the early 1950s, the athletic spirit at Rutgers was very high because most of the athletic programs were very successful. As a result of this new athletic spirit, RU's student body felt it was the right time to change the school nickname and mascot by making them more masculine to fit its new image. After the school organized a selection process and the votes were in, the Knights were chosen as the new nickname and mascot. Then in 1955, the name was changed to the Scarlet Knights. The new name and mascot rejuvenated athletics and school spirit at Rutgers University. Scarlet, RU's official school color, was first proposed to represent the school's official color in RU's newspaper (the *Targum*) in May 1869. The RU students chose scarlet because of its beauty and the easy accessibility of scarlet ribbons, which were used to show school spirit and support. In time, black was added as a background color.

SCHOOL NAME:	San Diego State University
NICKNAME:	Aztecs
MASCOT:	indian ("Monty Montezuma")
COLORS:	scarlet and black
CONFERENCE:	Mountain West Conference

HISTORY

The athletic teams at San Diego State University (SDSU) have not always been referred to as the Aztecs. Back in 1921, when SDSU first established athletic teams, the media often called the teams the Starters or the Professors. Then during the 1923–24 seasons, the *Paper Lion*, SDSU's newspaper, tried to promote the name Wampus Cats. In 1924, the *Paper Lion* organized a contest to choose a new nickname for SDSU, after athletic director C. E. Peterson felt it was time for a change. Some of the suggested names that were submitted to the newspaper and passed on to the selection committee were Panthers, Balboans, and Thoroughbreds. In 1925, the committee decided to override the list of suggestions and chose the name Aztecs. With SDSU being located in the Southwest, Aztecs seemed more appropriate for the image that SDSU was trying to portray. There was no animosity from students for the committee's choice. In February of that same year, SDSU president Hardy approved and adopted Aztecs as the official school nickname for SDSU.

To help uphold the strong Southwestern pride and image of SDSU, the school's rally committee wanted to create a college mascot that would be of historical significance to Montezuma II, the ruler of the Aztec empire during the early 1500s. As a result, Monty Montezuma was selected as the official school mascot for SDSU.

San Diego State College (now SDSU) was formed in 1921, when San Diego Normal School and San Diego Junior College decided to merge. Prior to the merging of these two schools, the normal school colors were white and gold, and the colors of the junior college were blue and gold. Upon merging, both schools compromised and chose white, gold, and blue as their official school colors. Then prior to the 1923–24 season, the school colors changed to purple and gold, but this presented a problem. You see, St. Augustine High School, which was also located in San Diego, also used the purple and gold colors. As a result, people could not distinguish between the sweaters worn by St. Augustine or San Diego State athletes. To make matters worse, Whittier College, a fierce conference competitor with San Diego State at the time, also used purple and gold. Additionally, the clothing manufacturing company that produced the Aztec merchandise for San Diego State could not guarantee the quality of the purple-colored products. With so many problems associated with the present school colors, associated student president Terrence Geddis led a school campaign to select new colors for San Diego State. When students finally got a chance to vote, the four colors that made it to the finalist list were green and gray, orange and gray, scarlet and black, and black and gold. In the end, scarlet and black were selected as the official school colors on January 19, 1928. San Diego State's new school colors made their debut on January 28, 1928, in a basketball game against Pomona College.

SCHOOL NAME: San Jose State University
NICKNAME: Spartans
MASCOT: spartan ("Sammy the Spartan")
COLORS: blue, gold, and gray
CONFERENCE: Mountain West Conference

HISTORY

Founded in 1857, San Jose State University (SJSU) was originally a college that trained elementary school teachers. Sometime after 1887, the school was named the State Normal School at San Jose. From 1887 to 1922, the school made many changes to its nickname and mascot. Changes to the nickname included the Daniels, the Teachers, the Pedagogues, the Normals, and the Normalites. When the school changed its name to SJSU in 1922, the Spartans and Sammy the Spartan became the official nickname and mascot for SJSU's athletic teams.

When the university was founded in 1857, the school colors were yellow and white. Sometime after that, the official school colors for SJSU's athletic teams were changed to its current colors of blue, gold, and gray. Unfortunately, there is no historical data explaining why those colors were chosen.

SCHOOL NAME:	Southern Methodist University
NICKNAME:	Mustangs
MASCOT:	mustang ("Peruna")
COLORS:	red and blue
CONFERENCE:	American Athletic Conference

HISTORY

When Southern Methodist University (SMU) first started competing in football, the school's teams were unofficially named the Parsons because of the high amount of theology students that were on the team. However, after the women's basketball team won a state championship, SMU officials decided that an official nickname and mascot were needed for the university. Members of the student body submitted a list of possible names, which included Bulls, Rams, Comanches, Bisons, Mustangs, Greyhounds, and Rattlers. When the list was narrowed down to three at a school pep rally held on October 17, 1917, the name Mustangs was chosen over Greyhounds and Bisons as the official nickname for SMU athletic teams.

Peruna, the name given to SMU's mustang mascot, was first seen by SMU fans on November 4, 1932, when the horse appeared at a football game. Peruna, which at the time was one of the most popular elixirs in Texas, was named the mascot after SMU student George Sexton was heard singing the words, "She'll be loaded with Peruna when she comes . . ." to the tune of "Comin' Around the Mountain."

President Hyer chose Harvard red and Yale blue as the official school colors for SMU to symbolize the high academic standards at SMU.

SCHOOL NAME:	Stanford University
NICKNAME:	Cardinal
MASCOT:	no official mascot
COLORS:	cardinal and white
CONFERENCE:	Pacific 12 Conference

HISTORY

On March 19, 1891, Stanford beat rival University of California at Berkeley (Cal) in its first ever big game. The next day, Stanford made cardinal red its official school color. When local newspapers became aware of the school's official color, they started referring to Stanford as the Cardinal. Stanford University athletic teams did not get their first official nickname until November 25, 1930. Back then, they were called the Indians. More than likely, that name, which was also the mascot for Stanford, was chosen because of the large Indian population that once inhabited the area. The Indian nickname was eventually dropped in 1972, after Stanford Native American students felt the mascot was an insult to their culture and heritage. From 1972 until 1981, Stanford's nickname was the Cardinals. That nickname was chosen to reference one of Stanford's official school colors, not the bird. Shortly after that, school president Donald Kennedy declared all Stanford athletic teams be nicknamed exclusively for their school color Cardinal.

Most people think a tree is the mascot for Stanford athletic teams. That is incorrect, because Stanford does not have an official mascot. The tree that is seen at sporting events is actually the mascot for the Stanford band. It represents El Palo Alto, the redwood tree that is the logo for the city of Palo Alto.

As previously mentioned, in 1891, Stanford chose cardinal red as its official school color after defeating Cal in its first ever big game. In 1940, the rules committee and the college conferences adopted a new rule, which required colleges football teams to have separate colors for their home and away jerseys. As a result, Stanford chose white as its second color.

SCHOOL NAME: Syracuse University
NICKNAME: Orangeman
MASCOT: orange ("Otto")
COLORS: orange and blue
CONFERENCE: Atlantic Coast Conference

HISTORY

To understand how Syracuse University (SU) derived its nickname, one would need to know how the school colors came about.

Back in 1872, SU chose the colors rose pink and pea green as their official school colors. This color combination was chosen because it represented the color of dawn. In 1889, after the visiting SU football team beat Hamilton College on their own turf, Hamilton students took out their frustration on SU players and fans by making fun of the team colors. Of course, this did not sit well with SU students. Therefore, a committee of students and faculty was formed to choose a new school color. In 1890, orange was chosen because the committee had discovered that no other school was using orange alone as their color. Soon after, all the men's varsity teams became known as the Orange or Orangemen. In 1898, blue became a background color when the alumni governors sanctioned a Syracuse flag of orange and blue, which at the time was a very popular color combination used by colleges. Eventfully, orange and blue were adopted as SU's official school colors.

For years, Syracuse University has been desperately searching for an official school mascot. SU's Saltine Warrior was forced to retire in 1978 because of a Native American student organization protest. This was followed by a slew of unsuccessful proposals: the Dome Ranger (an insurance agent in an orange cowboy outfit and blue mask), Dome Eddie (a gnat-like figure in orange sweats with Elton John glasses and an incandescent wig), and Beast from the East (an electric green monster). Eventually, Otto the Orange (a juiced-up, bumbling citrus fruit with arms and legs) found a home at Syracuse University. The concept for having an orange as an official mascot was quite simple. Since SU athletic teams are called the Orangemen or Orange, why not have an orange as a mascot?

In 1990, Otto was graced with his name by the SU cheerleading squad. After the first two oranges were dubbed Clyde and Woody, respectively, the pep squad had narrowed their choice down to two names: Opie or Otto. Upon further review, they chose Otto, fearing that the name Opie would lead to the inevitable rhyme with "dopey."

SCHOOL NAME:	Temple University
NICKNAME:	Owls
MASCOT:	owl
COLORS:	cherry and white
CONFERENCE:	American Athletic Conference

HISTORY

Since the founding of Temple University in the 1880s, the owl has always been the official nickname and mascot of the university for good reason. You see, besides Temple being the first university in the country to use an owl as an official mascot, it used to be a night school for low-income students. Russell Conwell, the founder of Temple University, encouraged his students to succeed by saying, "The owl of the night makes the eagle of the day." The owl was also chosen because it represents wisdom, knowledge, and is also the symbol for the Greek goddess Athena, who is the goddess of wisdom, arts, skills, and warfare. Besides the owl being a perceptive, resourceful, quick, and courageous creature, from an athletic point of view, it is also a fierce fighter.

In terms of official school colors, Temple University once again set a trend, this time for being the first college in the nation to use the color cherry in 1888. Red and white were and are still very common color combinations used by colleges. Temple University wanted to be unique so elected to replace red with the color cherry. Just how unique is this color combination? To date, besides Temple, the University of New Mexico is the only other school competing in Division I athletics that uses cherry as one of their school colors.

SCHOOL NAME:	Texas A&M University
NICKNAME:	Aggies
MASCOT:	collie ("Reveille")
COLORS:	maroon and white
CONFERENCE:	Southeastern Conference

HISTORY

Texas A&M University athletic teams are called the Aggies because that name is short for "agriculture." Originally, the school opened on October 4, 1876, and was called the Agricultural and Mechanical College of Texas, or A&M for short. Today, A&M does not stand for anything. For historical reasons, the school chose to keep them as part of their name.

Reveille IX, which is a full-blooded collie dog, is the official mascot for Texas A&M University. Also known as the Miss Rev, Reveille is the highest-ranking member of the school's corps of cadets. But why is a collie the school mascot? Well, back in January 1931, a group of cadets accidentally hit a small dog when returning from Navasota, Texas. Although pets were not allowed on campus, the cadets decided to sneak the dog into their dormitory room and nurse it back to health. But the next morning, the dog's cover was blown when it started barking at a bugler assigned to play reveille to wake the cadets. From that day forward, Reveille became the name of that dog, and the following football season, it became the official mascot for Texas A&M. Each game, Reveille would lead the band onto the field.

The official school colors for Texas A&M are maroon and white. Unfortunately, there is no historical data explaining why those colors were chosen.

SCHOOL NAME: Texas Christian University
NICKNAME: Horned Frogs
MASCOT: horned frog ("Super Frog")
COLORS: purple and white
CONFERENCE: Big 12 Conference

HISTORY

Back in 1871, Texas Christian University's (TCU) yearbook was called the *Horned Frog*. In time, the name was changed to plural (Horned Frogs) and became the official nickname for all TCU teams. The selection committee, which consisted of two library societies and the coach of the TCU football team, chose Horned Frogs because of the reptile's origin to the state of Texas. In 1980, Horned Frogs was selected as the number-one college nickname in the country by ESPN.

In 1896, the TCU Student Selections Committee chose purple and white as the official school colors for their athletic teams. Purple represented royalty, and white symbolized a "clean" game.

SCHOOL NAME:	Texas State University–San Marcos
NICKNAME:	Bobcats
MASCOT:	bobcat ("Boko")
COLORS:	maroon and gold
CONFERENCE:	Sun Belt Conference

HISTORY

Prior to 1919, Texas State University–San Marcos (Texas State), formally Southwest Texas Normal School, did not have a mascot and had unofficial nicknames for each of its individual athletic team. Those names included the Gypsies, the Nymphs, the Topsies, the Spirits, the Wonders, and the Goblins. When Normal athletic director Oscar Strahan arrived in 1919, he started a campaign to come up with a nickname and mascot as a way to raise school spirit. The student council formed a committee that was led by C. Spurgeon Smith, who was the head of Normal School's Biology Department. Smith had suggested Bobcats as the official nickname because that animal is indigenous to Central Texas and fights with great courage. The committee accepted Smith's suggestion and officially made Bobcats the nickname and mascot of Normal's athletic teams.

Although a bobcat was chosen as the official mascot, it did not have a name until 1964, when a Name the Bobcat contest was sponsored by Phi Delta Gamma sorority, now Alpha Xi Delta. A sophomore student named Beth Greenless had submitted the name Boko, and that name was selected from over one hundred submittals. Normal's first Boko mascot was a real bobcat, but then the school decided to use a costumed mascot instead of a live animal. Over the years, Boko has gone through a lot of changes. The most recent change occurred in 2003, when Southwest Texas Normal School's name was changed to Texas State University.

The official school colors of Texas State's athletic teams are maroon and gold. Those colors were derived from the school's flower, which is the gaillardia. The gaillardia is a wildflower that is native to the state of Texas.

SCHOOL NAME:	Texas Tech University
NICKNAME:	Red Raiders
MASCOT:	masked raider
COLORS:	scarlet and black
CONFERENCE:	Big 12 Conference

HISTORY

On March 15, 1926, the students of Texas Tech University voted to have the Matadors be the school's official nickname and the colors scarlet and black as the official colors. Even though the students selected the colors, it was Mrs. Ewing Young Freeland, the wife of Texas Tech's football coach, who came up with the nickname. Her idea was influenced by the Spanish architecture that surrounds the campus. But in 1936, Tech students voted to change the school nickname to the Red Raiders after reflecting back on an article written by *Lubbock Avalanche-Journal* sportswriter Collier Parris describing the 1932 Texas Tech versus New Mexico football game. With Tech having a strong season and wearing red uniforms, he wrote, "The Red Raiders from Texas Tech, terror of the Southwest this year, swooped in the New Mexico University camp today." After four years, Red Raiders caught on, and the old nickname faded into history.

Since September 26, 1936, Tech students started the tradition of having a masked rider on a horse wearing black riding clothes, a red cape, and a bolero hat to enhance school spirit and pride. They would mysteriously appear during home football games, circle the field, and then disappear for the remainder of the game. Back then, the person on the horse was called a Ghost Rider because nobody knew his identity. They are now the new and improved Masked Rider and continue to carry on the school's great tradition.

The official school colors of Texas Tech athletic teams are scarlet and black. Unfortunately, there is no historical data explaining why those colors were chosen.

SCHOOL NAME: Troy University
NICKNAME: Trojans
MASCOT: trojan ("T-Roy")
COLORS: cardinal, silver, and black
CONFERENCE: Sun Belt Conference

HISTORY

When Troy University's football team first started competing against other schools in the 1910s, their nickname was the Bulldogs or the Teachers, since the school was originally a teachers college. Then in 1922, the nickname was changed to the Trojans for the first time. Upon the arrival of Albert Elmore, who became Troy University's new football coach in 1931, he changed the name to the Red Wave. Elmore chose that name because it was a variation of the University of Alabama's nickname, the Crimson Tide, which also happened to be his alma mater. Then in 1973, Troy University's student body voted to change the nickname back to the Trojans just hours before the football team played an away game against Northeast Louisiana (now Louisiana-Monroe), which resulted in a 15–15 tie.

In the mid-1980, the student body decided to vote on a name for the Trojan mascot. At the conclusion of the naming contest, the name T-Roy was the winner.

The official school colors for Troy University's athletic teams are cardinal, silver, and black. Unfortunately, there is no historical data explaining why those colors were chosen.

SCHOOL NAME:	Tulane University
NICKNAME:	Green Wave
MASCOT:	pelican ("Rip Tide")
COLORS:	olive green and sky blue
CONFERENCE:	American Athletic Conference

HISTORY

From 1893 to 1923, Tulane University (TU) student newspapers (*Tulane Weekly* and *Tulane Hullabaloo*) called its sports teams the Olive and Blue, and Greenbacks. Then on October 20, 1920, *Tulane Hullabaloo*'s editor Earl Sparling wrote a football song and printed it in the paper. The song was titled "The Rolling Green Wave." Then on November 19, 1920, the *Tulane Hullabaloo* wrote an article about the Tulane versus Mississippi A&M game and referred to the team as the Green Wave. By the end of the season, the *Tulane Hullabaloo*, along with many other newspapers, was calling TU sports teams the Green Wave. However, the Greenback nickname was still being used until 1923.

TU chose to have a pelican as its official mascot because the pelican is the state bird for Louisiana. In the 1940s and 1950s, TU had a live pelican mascot. Sometime after that, the school decided to replace a live bird with a costumed pelican. TU's mascot is named Rip Tide and was selected by the school's administration.

The official school colors of TU's athletic teams are olive green and sky blue. Unfortunately, there is no historical data explaining why those colors were chosen.

SCHOOL NAME: United States Air Force Academy
NICKNAME: Falcons
MASCOT: gyrfalcon ("Aurora, the Bird")
COLORS: blue and silver
CONFERENCE: Mountain West Conference

HISTORY

On September 25, 1955, members of the cadet wings (class of 1959) at the United States Air Force Academy (Air Force) chose the nickname Falcons to represent their athletic teams. The falcon was chosen because they felt as though its flight characteristics symbolized the role of the United States Air Force. Some of those characteristics were speed, power, and grace in flight, courage, keen eyesight, and alertness. The falcon also personified the behaviors sought in Air Force Academy cadets, such as courage, intelligence, love of the wild sky, ferocity in attack but gentleness in response, and discipline.

Aurora, or the Bird, is a gyrfalcon and the mascot for Air Force. The gyrfalcon is a bird of prey and the largest of the falcon species. In addition to making its home in northern North America, the gyrfalcon can be found in Europe and Asia.

Blue and gray were chosen as the official colors for Air Force. Blue represents the sky, and silver represents lightning.

SCHOOL NAME:	United States Military Academy
NICKNAME:	Black Knights
MASCOT:	mule ("Ranger III, Stryker, and Raider")
COLORS:	black, gray, and gold
CONFERENCE:	NCAA Division FBS Independents Conference

HISTORY

The nickname for the United States Military Academy (Army) athletic teams is the Black Knights because of the color of their uniforms.

A mule was chosen as the official mascot for Army because of its long historical use in military operations for hauling guns, supplies, and ammunition. The mule is also the symbol for the corps of cadets. There are three mules that serve as the official mascots for West Point: Ranger III, Stryker, and Raider.

The official school colors for Army athletic teams are black, gray, and gold. Those colors were chosen because they represent the components of gunpowder, which are charcoal (black), saltpeter (potassium nitrate) gray, and sulfur (gold).

SCHOOL NAME: United States Naval Academy
NICKNAME: Midshipmen
MASCOT: goat ("Bill")
COLORS: navy blue and gold
CONFERENCE: American Athletic Conference

HISTORY

The nickname for all athletic teams at the United States Naval Academy (Navy) is the Midshipmen. So what exactly is a midshipman? The word "midshipsman" was first used in seventeenth-century English by sailors to designate those men who were stationed in the middle portion of the vessel. By 1687, the second *s* was dropped, which changed the meaning of the word. Midshipmen were young boys, sometimes as young as seven or eight, who were apprenticed to sea captains to learn the sailor's trade. In the early establishment of the American Navy, midshipmen trained on board ships until they were commissioned as ensigns. When the United States Naval Academy was founded in 1845, it became possible, as it is today, for midshipmen to enter the Navy directly from civilian life. To date, the word "midshipmen" refers to students attending the United States Naval Academy.

The mascot for Navy is a goat for good reason. Over two hundred years ago, goats were an integral part of Navy life. They were used as livestock on ships to provide sailors with food, milk, eggs, and in some cases, pets. The name of Navy's mascot is Bill. More than likely, this name was selected because it's short for "billy goat," which is a male goat.

In 1892, the United States Naval Academy adopted navy blue and gold as the school's official colors. The class of 1890 takes credit for this happening. You see, back when the naval academy was first founded, each class had its own colors. The class of 1890 chose navy blue and gold as their class colors. In doing so, a decision was made by all midshipmen to make navy blue and gold the naval academy's official colors as well.

SCHOOL NAME:	University of Akron
NICKNAME:	Zips
MASCOT:	kangaroo ("Zippy")
COLORS:	blue and gold
CONFERENCE:	Mid-American Conference

HISTORY

In 1935, the University of Akron (UA) decided to hold a contest to decide on a nickname for all of its athletic teams. Students, faculty, and alumni were all involved in this selection process. Names that were submitted included Golden Blue Devils, Tip Toppers, Rubbernecks, Hillbillies, Kangaroos, and the Chevaliers. At the conclusion of this event, freshman Margaret Hamlin was declared the winner for submitting the name Zippers. She received ten dollars, a pair of six-dollar overshoes, and a brand name of the BF Goodrich Company. In 1950, athletic director Kenneth "Red" Cochran officially shortened the name to Zips.

On May 1, 1953, Zippy the Kangaroo became the official mascot for the UA. All-American diver Bob Savoy, who was the chairman of the committee involved in the mascot selection process, was the person who made that recommendation to student council. At first, there was resentment by some of the students at the university because they were not involved in the selection process. However, after defenders of the mascot pointed out that the kangaroo is an animal that is "fast, agile, and powerful, with underlying determination, all the necessary qualities of an athlete," Zippy was accepted by all UA students.

Blue and gold were adopted as UA's official school colors back when the university was known as Buchtel College in the 1880s. There are references to the colors in an 1890 article put out by the school newspaper, but the reason those colors were chosen is still unknown. The school was renamed the University of Akron in 1913.

SCHOOL NAME:	University of Alabama
NICKNAME:	Crimson Tide
MASCOT:	elephant
COLORS:	crimson and white
CONFERENCE:	Southeastern Conference

HISTORY

In the early days of college football, the University of Alabama football team was simply known as the Crimson White or the Thin Red Line. Both of these names were derived from the school's colors. In 1907, a sportswriter named Hugh Roberts thought of the name Crimson Tide when describing an Alabama versus Auburn game being played "in a sea of mud" on a wet red clay field in Birmingham, Alabama. The Thin Red Line played a great game and resulted in the heavily favored Auburn having to settle for a 6–6 tie. The name Crimson Tide was eventually adopted as the school's official nickname after a sports editor from the *Birmingham News* named Zipp Newman popularized the name by repeatedly using it in his column.

Although the University of Alabama's nickname is the Crimson Tide, its official mascot is an elephant. The school's 1930 national championship football team takes the credit for this happening. Coach Wade's team was most feared and recognized for its brutal front line that was big, tough, fast, and aggressive. In turn, these characteristics were recognized by an excited fan who shouted from the stands at the end of the quarter of the Alabama versus Mississippi game, "Hold your horses, the elephants are coming!" Everett Strupper, a sportswriter from the *Atlanta Journal*, witnessed this and started referring to the Alabama linemen as the Red Elephants, the color being in reference to their crimson jerseys. The name continued to be used by other sportswriters, and the concept of a red elephant mascot fared well with the university. After all, it would have been rather difficult to try to construct a crimson tide costume.

Although there is no confirmed documentation to support this concept, it is believed that crimson was chosen by the University of Alabama as its official school color to proudly signify the beautiful fertile red clay soil that is found throughout the state of Alabama. White was chosen as the secondary color.

SCHOOL NAME:	University of Alabama at Birmingham
NICKNAME:	Blazers
MASCOT:	dragon ("Blaze")
COLORS:	green and gold
CONFERENCE:	Conference USA

HISTORY

Although the University of Alabama at Birmingham (UAB) has been a full-fledged university since the late 1960s, the school did not start competing in intercollegiate athletics until 1977. A decision was made to hold a contest on campus to determine a nickname for UAB athletic teams. The event was advertised in the *Kaleidoscope*, UAB's newspaper. Some of the potential names that were submitted were the Barons (a tribute to the city's industrial heritage and the name of Birmingham's AA baseball team), Titans, Warriors, and Blazers. At the conclusion of the event, Blazers was chosen as the official nickname. Rumor has it that Blazers was chosen for one or two reasons. The first being UAB having a reputation for trailblazing in the medical field by having a world-class medical center and one of the nation's top medical schools. The second, 1977 was also the year that the Portland Trailblazers won the NBA Championship.

The search for an official mascot became much more challenging. Between the late 1970s and the mid-1990s, UAB had several mascots: a dragon; a rooster named Beauregard T. Rooster; Blaze, who was a fierce-looking Nordic warrior that made his debut at the inception of UAB's football program; and finally, another dragon that went by the name Blaze in 1995. The dragon replaced the Nordic warrior after the school started receiving complaints about his evil look.

The year 1977 was also the year that forest green and old gold became UAB's official school colors. Those colors were chosen by a student and faculty vote.

SCHOOL NAME:	University of Arizona
NICKNAME:	Wildcats
MASCOT:	wildcat ("Wilbur" and "Wilma")
COLORS:	cardinal red and navy blue
CONFERENCE:	Pacific 12 Conference

HISTORY

In the early 1900s, the University of Arizona (UA) football team was not very good, and their record showed it. However, in 1914, all that changed. Under new head coach James Fred McKale, UA's football team performed so well against Occidental College, which was a West Coast powerhouse, that Los Angeles reporter Bill Henry wrote in his sports article, "The Arizona men showed the fight of Wildcats." The UA student body immediately fell in love with that name and made Wildcats the school's official nickname.

UA's first mascot was an actual bobcat that was a gift from the freshman football team in 1915. His name was Rufus Arizona, after UA president Rufus B. von KleinSmid. In 1959, UA's first costumed mascot, Wilbur, was introduced at the UA versus Texas Tech football game. He was so entertaining to the crowd that he accompanied the team on the road the following week. In 1986, Wilbur married his longtime girlfriend Wilma, and the two of them became the official mascots for the University of Arizona.

UA's original colors were sage green and silver, but the school's equipment manager was trying to buy new uniforms, and the only uniforms that were affordable were red and blue. Therefore, UA changed its official colors to red and blue.

SCHOOL NAME:	University of Arkansas
NICKNAME:	Razorbacks
MASCOT:	razorback ("Tusk")
COLORS:	cardinal and white
CONFERENCE:	Southeastern Conference

HISTORY

When the University of Arkansas first started competing in intercollegiate athletics, the school's athletic teams were called the Cardinals. However, on October 30, 1909, after University of Arkansas coach Hugo Bezdek guided his team to a 16–0 victory over Louisiana State University, he referred to his players as "a wild band of razorback hogs" because of their tenacious wild fighting ability. Keeping this idea in his mind, Bezdek continued to refer to his players as Razorbacks. As a result, the new nickname became increasingly popular. So in 1910, the student body voted to change the official university nickname and mascot from the Cardinals to the Razorbacks. Then in the 1920s, the University of Arkansas adopted the "Wooo, Pig, Sooie" school yell: more commonly known today as the Call of the Hogs.

Cardinal and white were chosen as the official school colors for the University of Arkansas since the athletic teams had previously been nicknamed the Cardinals and since the cardinal bird was the school's official mascot. White was chosen as the secondary color.

SCHOOL NAME: University of Buffalo
NICKNAME: Bulls
MASCOT: bull ("Victor E. Bull")
COLORS: blue and white
CONFERENCE: Mid-American Conference

HISTORY

The official nickname for the University of Buffalo (UB) athletic teams is the Bulls. Although there is no historical documentation explaining why that name was chosen, buffalo were once indigenous to upstate New York. This could be the reason behind the Bulls (the name for a male buffalo) nickname.

In 1934, UB's first unofficial mascot was a bison head named Boscoe. In 1957, UB's first live mascot was a black angus Irish Dexter named Buster. Dexters are miniature cattle that originated from Ireland. UB continued to use live Dexters (all named Buster) until 1970, when UB discontinued its NCAA Division I football program. However, at the Division III level, the football and basketball teams elected to use a costumed bull mascot named Buster. In 1997, in preparation for returning to Division I athletic competition, the UB athletic department held a Name the Mascot contest. UB student Rustie Hill won that contest for submitting the name Victor E. Bull. Shortly after that, the department introduced Victor E. Bull (an anthropomorphic bull) as its official mascot.

The official school colors for UB athletic teams are blue and white. Those colors were chosen back in 1886, forty years after its medical school was established. At that time, the medical school was using white ribbons to tie their diplomas. As a way to distinguish itself from the medical school and in preparation for its first graduating class, the School of Pharmacy decided to tie blue ribbons on their diplomas. As other departments were established and the student population increased, UB needed to create a spirit insignia. Blue and white were chosen because that color combination represents the exciting and persistent nature of UB, as well as its storied history and demanding academic standards.

SCHOOL NAME: University of California at Berkeley
NICKNAME: The Golden Bears
MASCOT: golden bear ("Oski")
COLORS: blue and gold
CONFERENCE: Pacific 12 Conference

HISTORY

In 1895, the first University of California (Cal) sports team to compete out of the state was the track team. For fans to recognize what state the team came from, the team elected to carry a banner displaying California's state emblem, the golden bear. The track team won several events, and as a result, the Golden Bears became the nickname for all Cal sports teams.

Prior to 1940, Cal used live bears as their mascot. However, in 1940, the school decided that was not a very good idea so elected to instead use a costumed mascot. The Oski Committee, which was a governing body that took care of the Cal bear, decided to dub the school's new mascot the same name. The name Oski was derived from Cal's popular "Oski Wow-Wow" yell.

In 1873, blue and gold were chosen as the official school colors for Cal. The blue represented the California sky, ocean, and the Yale University graduates that helped establish the University of California. The gold symbolizes California's state animal, the golden bear.

SCHOOL NAME:	University of California at Los Angeles
NICKNAME:	Bruins
MASCOT:	bruin ("Joe")
COLORS:	sky blue and gold
CONFERENCE:	Pacific 12 Conference

HISTORY

Prior to the University of California at Los Angeles (UCLA) using a bruin (a brown bear) as its nickname and mascot, they were called the Cubs. Then in 1924, UCLA adopted the Grizzly Bear. However, in 1926, UCLA decided to once again change their nickname and mascot because at that time, Pacific 10 rival, University of Montana, also utilized the Grizzly Bear to represent its teams. After an intense search was organized, UCLA decided to use one of the University of California at Berkeley's two nicknames, the Bruins. From that time on, all UCLA teams have been called the Bruins and use Joe the Bruin as their official school mascot.

In discussing the official school colors for UCLA, it should be pointed out that all University of California campuses use variations of blue and yellow. For UCLA, the school's athletic teams are represented by the colors sky blue and gold. The blue symbolizes the ocean, the local wild flowers, and the blue uniforms worn by school's cadet corps. The yellow honors California as the Golden State, the California golden poppy, and California's golden sunsets.

SCHOOL NAME: University of Central Florida
NICKNAME: Golden Knights
MASCOT: golden knight ("Knightro")
COLORS: black and gold
CONFERENCE: American Athletic Conference

HISTORY

In the summer of 1970, students at Florida Technological University (now the University of Central Florida) got together and approached school president Charles Millican for suggestions on determining an official school mascot for the university. As a result, Operation Mascot was formed. There were both suggestion boxes and a committee made up of students, staff, and faculty members. After a long tedious process of gathering information and determining which student suggestions should be considered in the final voting process, the winning entry was announced that December. In the end, the committee chose the Knights of Pegasus and associated the mascot and nickname with the university seal, which displays Pegasus, the winged horse of Greek mythology. Eight years later, the university changed its name to the University of Central Florida (UCF). Then in 1993, UCF's nickname and mascot were changed to the Golden Knights by a man named Steve Sloan, who was the UCF athletic director.

Like the official school mascot and nickname, the UCF official school colors came from the university seal, which is black and gold.

SCHOOL NAME: University of Cincinnati
NICKNAME: Bearcat
MASCOT: bearcat
COLORS: red and black
CONFERENCE: American Athletic Conference

HISTORY

Historically, there are three possible versions of how the University of Cincinnati (UC) came up with the Bearcat nickname. The first version was that in 1914, a cartoon or picture was published showing UC Lineman Leonard K. "Teddy" Baer standing on a football field next to a Stutz Bearcat automobile. The second version states that the nickname was the result of a sports cartoon that appeared in the newspaper following a 1914 Cincinnati versus Kentucky game showing a wildcat being harassed by a catlike animal. The last version traces the name to a 1912 newspaper account of a UC game in which *Cincinnati Enquirer* sports editor Jack Ryder wrote that the team played like bearcats.

The story is very vague in terms of how UC derived its school colors. However, apparently, back in the 1900s, each class had its own set of colors. In 1906, this eventually resulted in UC deciding to use the red-and-black color combination as its official school colors.

SCHOOL NAME:	University of Colorado
NICKNAME:	Buffalos
MASCOT:	buffalo ("Ralphie")
COLORS:	silver and gold
CONFERENCE:	Pacific 12 Conference

HISTORY

Prior to 1934, the University of Colorado (CU) athletic teams did not have a nickname, so the teams were sometimes referred to as the Silver and Gold, Silver Helmets, Yellow Jackets, Hornets, Arapahoes, Big Horns, Grizzlies, and Frontiersmen. Subsequently, in the fall of 1934, CU's newspaper announced that there would be a contest to pick an official nickname for CU sports teams. The winner would receive five dollars. Students Claude Bates and James Profit were cowinners for submitting Buffalos as the school's nickname.

Three weeks after the name Buffalos was selected as the official nickname, a real buffalo appeared at a CU football game. Some students paid twenty-five dollars to rent a buffalo calf and a real cowboy to be the animal's keeper. This concept was an instant success with the CU students. The first official buffalo mascot was given to the university by Mahlon White. His name was Mr. Chips, and he would regularly appear at all CU home games through the 1950s. CU was without a mascot for quite a few years, until Ralphie made her first appearance in 1966. Since that time, more buffalos have been used to continue the CU tradition of leading CU football teams out onto the field at the start of the first and second half of home games.

In 1888, silver and gold were chosen as the official school colors for CU. Those colors were chosen because they represent the state of Colorado's silver and gold mineral wealth. Black was added to the uniforms in the 1950s as an accent color.

SCHOOL NAME:	University of Connecticut
NICKNAME:	Huskies
MASCOT:	husky ("Jonathan the Husky")
COLORS:	navy blue, white, and gray
CONFERENCE:	American Athletic Conference

HISTORY

Prior to 1933, the University of Connecticut (UCONN) was called the Connecticut Agricultural College, and its athletic teams were referred to as the Aggies. In 1933, the school changed its name for the second time. The new name was now the Connecticut State College. In 1934, the school's newspaper, the *Daily Campus*, conducted a student body poll to change the name of its athletic teams. The students chose the name Huskies. Five years later, the school changed its name for the third and final time to the University of Connecticut.

In 1934, the University of Rhode Island's mascot, which is a ram, was kidnapped. That incident caught the attention of Connecticut State College, and the student body decided it wanted to have its own live mascot. In January 1935, the first husky mascot arrived at Connecticut State College. A Name the Mascot contest was organized by the alumni association, and the winning name was Jonathan. That name was chosen in honor of Jonathan Trumbull, who was the only man to serve as governor in both the English colony and an American state (Connecticut). All of UCONN's past and present mascots have and will always be named Jonathan. UCONN has both a canine and costumed Jonathan mascot.

The official school colors for UCONN are navy blue, white, and gray. There are two unofficial reasons explaining why blue and white were chosen. The first reason being that those two colors were adopted from the Connecticut state flag. The second, a student's organization in 1896 or 1897 chose blue because it represents the sky, and white, the clouds. As for the color gray, that is a secondary color that was added years later.

SCHOOL NAME:	University of Florida
NICKNAME:	Gators
MASCOT:	alligator ("Albert and Alberta")
COLORS:	orange and blue
CONFERENCE:	Southeastern Conference

HISTORY

The University of Florida (UF) athletic teams are called the Gators. The person responsible for coining that name was Austin Miller, who was a native of Gainesville and set up a law practice after graduating from the University of Virginia (UVA) in Charlottesville in 1910. When Austin was still attending UVA in 1907, his father decided to pay him a visit. While in Charlottesville, the elder Miller, who owned a drug and stationary store in Gainesville, a popular hangout spot for university students, decided to order some pennants and banners for UF (at that time was called the University of Gainesville) from the Michie Company, which was engaged in the manufacture of such items. It was important for his father to order these items because 1907 was the year the university had fielded its first team. While in the store, the Millers saw pennants that read "Yale Bulldogs," "Princeton Tigers," and other school emblems. When the Michie manager asked the Millers what Florida's emblem was, Austin's father realized that the school didn't have one. Austin decided to choose the name Alligators as the university's emblem for two reasons: The first is because the alligator is a native animal to the state of Florida. The second is because the store manager informed Austin that no other school at that time was using the alligator name. Without knowing if the name would be accepted by the Gainesville student body, Austin's father placed an order to have the store manager make the pennants bearing the Alligators name as soon as possible in preparation for the 1908 school term.

UF's first mascot was a live alligator named Albert, who made his first debut at a 1957 sporting event. From 1957 to 1969, UF used several different alligators and, at one point, even used a mechanical reptile. In 1970, the school decided to replace a live Albert alligator with a full-body vinyl-costumed Albert. Then in 1986, Alberta the Alligator was introduced as Albert's sidekick and friend.

Prior to UF being established in 1853, the university's two primary competitors were the University of Florida at Lake City, whose colors are blue and white; and the East Florida Seminary, whose colors are orange and black. It is believed that as a tribute to those institutions, UF chose the color combination orange and blue from those two schools as its official school colors.

SCHOOL NAME:	University of Georgia
NICKNAME:	Bulldogs
MASCOT:	bulldog ("UGA")
COLORS:	red and black
CONFERENCE:	Southeastern Conference

HISTORY

How did the University of Georgia (UGA) derive its Bulldog nickname? Many people believe that Abraham Baldwin, who was UGA's first president and a Yale University alumnus, copied the nickname from his alma mater. As a show of support for that nickname, a sportswriter for the *Atlanta Journal* named Morgan Blake wrote an article on November 3, 1920, and stated that "the Georgia Bulldog would sound good because there is a certain dignity about a bulldog, as well as ferocity." Furthermore, on November 6, 1920, Cliff Wheatley, who was also a sportswriter, used the Bulldog nickname five times when describing a UGA football game. Consequently, that name has been used ever since.

UGA (University of Georgia) is the name of the school's mascot. The solid white English bulldog is one of the best known college mascots in the country and has been making appearances at UGA events since his inception in 1956.

Although there is no historical data that explains why UGA chose red and black as its official school colors, one possibility is that red was chosen because, story has it, when a Georgia Bulldog smells a Georgia Tech Yellow Jacket, he sees red. Black was likely chosen as a complementary color.

SCHOOL NAME:	University of Hawaii
NICKNAME:	Rainbows
MASCOT:	rainbow warrior ("Kamahameha the Great")
COLORS:	green and white
CONFERENCE:	Mountain West Conference

HISTORY

Prior to the University of Hawaii (UH) taking on the nickname of the Rainbows, all their teams were known as the Deans. However, when a rainbow suddenly appeared over the field in what was the final football game of the 1923 season against Oregon State, many fans believed that it was the rainbow that resulted in UH beating highly favored Oregon State by a score of 7–0. Furthermore, when you consider the fact that many Hawaiian chiefs and locals believed that rainbows possess certain magical powers, the sighting of the rainbow just added confirmation to this spectacular story. After sportswriters started referring to UH teams as the Rainbows, the name was adopted as the official nickname for all UH teams.

The rainbow warrior, Kamahameha the Great, was chosen as the official mascot for UH for historical and financial reasons. In historical terms, it was Kamahameha's great strength, skill, and fighting spirit that enabled the Hawaiian Islands to become united. Financially, the nickname provides tremendous support for the UH scholarship fund-raising organization, Ahahui Koa Anuenue, which means "the Order of the Rainbow Warrior."

Green and white were chosen as the official school colors for UH because a group of the faculty's wives came to the conclusion that certain colors would not be made available for decorations and color schemes for the school's social calendar. You see, because of Hawaii's status as an island, materials would sometimes take weeks to arrive from the mainland. Therefore, the wives decided to use basic white because it was always available, and green decorations could be provided because of Hawaii's tropical plants. Later it was found out that green represents the color of Lono, the ancient Hawaiian god of agriculture. White also signifies Hawaiian royalty and symbolizes "the best and the finest." As a result, the faculty chose green and white as the official school colors for UH.

SCHOOL NAME: University of Houston
NICKNAME: Cougars
MASCOT: cougar ("Shasta")
COLORS: scarlet red and albino white
CONFERENCE: American Athletic Conference

HISTORY

Since 1927, the official nickname for University of Houston (Houston) athletic teams is the Cougars. The name was chosen by John R. Bender, who was an early physical education instructor at Houston and the former head football coach at Washington State University (WSU). While at WSU, Mr. Bender became quite fond of their mascot, which was a cougar. When he arrived at Houston, the school's first extracurricular activity was a school newspaper, and students were looking for a name. Mr. Bender suggested naming it the Cougar, because the cougar embodies grace, power, and pride. The Cougar name was unanimously accepted, and became the official school nickname.

Houston's mascot is Shasta the Cougar. Shasta made her debut back on October 17, 1947, when the Alpha Phi Omega fraternity purchased her from a wild animal rancher named Manuel King. From 1947 to 1989, there have been five Shasta cougars that have represented Houston athletic teams. After Shasta V passed away in 1989, Houston decided to do away with live cougar mascots and replace them with a costumed student.

The official school colors for Houston are scarlet red and albino white. Those colors came from Sam Houston's (president of the Republic of Texas) ancestor, Sir Hugh. Scarlet Red symbolizes blood being the life source of the soul and represents the fact that Sir Hugh's actions saved a bloodline of royalty. Consequently, it symbolizes courage and perseverance. Albino white symbolizes the purity and perfections of a heart, mind, and soul that are dedicated to serve faithfully. It also symbolizes helping others and compassion.

SCHOOL NAME:	University of Illinois
NICKNAME:	Fighting Illini
MASCOT:	indian ("Chief Illiniwek")
COLORS:	orange and blue
CONFERENCE:	Big Ten Conference

HISTORY

The University of Illinois (UI) chose the nickname Fighting Illini in honor of the Illiniwek Indians, which was an American Indian tribe that once lived in the region. In time, the French settlers changed the name to Illinois, which is how the state got its name.

Chief Illiniwek emerged as the UI mascot when Robert Zuppke, a former UI football coach, discovered that Illiniwek, when translated, means "they are men." Therefore, in 1926, Chief Illiniwek made his debut when Ray Dvorak, who was the UI assistant band director, convinced the UI administration to allow an American Indian to dance during halftime of the Illinois versus Pennsylvania football game. Lester Leutwiler, a UI student interested in American Indian traditions, was chosen for the role.

Prior to 1894, the official school colors for UI were silver and cardinal and then Dartmouth green. Silver and cardinal were selected by the students, and Dartmouth green was chosen by E. K. Hall, UI's former athletic director. He chose that color in honor of his alma mater, Dartmouth College. However, in 1894, UI's president convinced the student body to change the school colors to orange and blue. Those colors signify the sun rising into the blue Midwest sky. Moreover, blue represents authority, power, loyalty, and integrity. Orange represents creativity, determination, and success.

SCHOOL NAME: University of Iowa
NICKNAME: Hawkeyes
MASCOT: "Herky the Hawk"
COLORS: gold and black
CONFERENCE: Big Ten Conference

HISTORY

The University of Iowa (UI) athletic teams are known as the Hawkeyes because Iowa is known as the Hawkeye State. The state name came from a fictional character in the book *Last of the Mohicans,* which was published in 1826. Judge David Rorer and James G. Edwards, who were the owner and editor of a newspaper company, which they named the Hawk-Eye, campaigned to popularize the state name. As a result, in 1838, Hawkeye became the state's official nickname.

In 1948, UI introduced Herky the Hawk as the school's mascot. Richard Spencer III, who was a journalism instructor, created the mascot, which was originally a cartoon character that he drew. The mascot's nickname was determined after the UI athletic department decided to hold a statewide contest. The mascot, which was originally a real hawk, made its first debut on October 5, 1956, at UI's first rally of the season. Eventually, Herky the Hawk transformed from an actual bird to a student dressed in a costume. The costumed Herky made its debut at a football game in 1959.

UI did not have official school colors for forty years. But in 1887, all that changed, thanks to a group of students who decided to choose the colors old gold and black. Gold represents Iowa's vast cornfields, and black, the state's rich soil.

SCHOOL NAME:	University of Kansas
NICKNAME:	Jayhawks
MASCOT:	jayhawk ("Jay")
COLORS:	crimson and blue
CONFERENCE:	Big 12 Conference

HISTORY

Since about the late 1880s, all the University of Kansas (KU) athletic teams have been called the Jayhawks. If one were to look back on history and find just how this nickname came about, it would make for some interesting reading.

For starters, a jayhawk is a fictitious bird. The name, which was a term used from Illinois to Texas to describe the characteristics of Kansas Settlers, combines two birds: the blue jay, a loud and belligerent bird known to rob other nests; and the sparrow hawk, a stealthy hunter. In other words, this term means "don't turn your back on this bird."

During this period, the Kansas territory was filled with jayhawks. The reason being that the state was divided in two because of political reasons. Half the settlers wanted a state where slavery would be legal, and the other half were hoping for a free state. This divided tension among settlers resulted in mass looting, cattle rustling, horse stealing, and attacks on each other's settlements. For a while, both groups of settlers were referred to as Jayhawks, but in the end, the free skilled staters coined the name after Kansas governor Charles Robinson put together a regiment called the Independent Mounted Kansas Jayhawks, which was put in place to help eliminate slavery and make Kansas a free state. To add, since Lawrence, Kansas, which is also the home of KU, was very much in favor of the free state philosophy, the name Jayhawks eventually became the nickname for all KU athletic teams in 1890. This was the same year that football was first introduced to the University of Kansas.

In the mid-1880s, the board of regents at KU adopted the color combination of maize and blue from the University of Michigan as the official school colors. However, when football arrived in 1890, KU officials wanted to change the color to Harvard University's crimson, in honor of Col. John J. Macon, a Harvard alumnus who donated money to the KU athletic field. When KU faculty that was alumni of Yale University got wind of this, they insisted that KU keep blue as the other color to show their lineage to Yale. So in 1896, the combination crimson and blue was officially chosen.

SCHOOL NAME:	University of Kentucky
NICKNAME:	Wildcats
MASCOT:	wildcat
COLORS:	blue and white
CONFERENCE:	Southeastern Conference

HISTORY

The official nickname for all athletic teams at the University of Kentucky (UK) is the Wildcats. A man by the name of Commandant Carbusier (head of the military department) was responsible for inspiring the Wildcat nickname when he told the State University (the former name of UK) football team that they had "fought like wildcats," following their 6–2 win over Illinois on October 9, 1909. In time, the Wildcat name became so popular with UK students, fans and the media that the UK student body decided to adopt Wildcats as the school's official nickname and mascot.

The official school colors for UK have not always been blue and white. Years ago, the UK student body had decided on blue and yellow prior to the Kentucky versus Centre College football game, which was played on December 19, 1891. The particular shade of blue used by UK was chosen when an inquisitive student who attended the school color selection meeting asked the question, "What color blue?" Richard C. Stoll, who was a football player for UK (from 1889 to 1994) responded to the question by pulling off his necktie and holding it up. The color of his tie, which was very close to royal blue, was the color selected by the committee. One year later, the UK student body dropped the color yellow in favor of white.

SCHOOL NAME: University of Louisiana–Lafayette
NICKNAME: Ragin Cajuns
MASCOT: pepper ("Cayenne")
COLORS: vermilion red and white
CONFERENCE: Sun Belt Conference

HISTORY

The University of Louisiana–Lafayette (ULL) sports teams have been competing in intercollegiate athletics since 1909, but its sports teams were without a nickname until the 1960s. The school was originally called the University of Southwestern Louisiana, and its football team was called the Bulldogs. Then in 1963, Coach Russ Fauikinberry changed the name to the Ragin Cajuns. Coach Faulkinberry chose this name because it's how he described his football players. The name also sat well with the area residents because ULL is located in Acadiana, Louisiana, which also happens to be the location where Cajuns originated. In the 1970s, Bob Henderson, who was ULL's sports information director, started using the name as a way to honor the sport teams and the Cajun heritage. As a result, in 1974, Ragin Cajuns became the official nickname for all ULL sports teams.

ULL students chose Cayenne the Pepper as it official mascot because cayenne represents the Ragin Cajun way of life, which is hot spicy food and unique music.

Vermilion red and white have been ULL's official school colors since 1898. Vermilion red was chosen because that color represents ULL's sprit, passion, and spice. White is the secondary color. UL Lafayette is the only university with vermilion as its official color. For many of their audiences, these colors are the most identifiable components of the school's brand.

SCHOOL NAME: University of Louisville
NICKNAME: Cardinals
MASCOT: cardinal
COLORS: cardinal red and black
CONFERENCE: Atlantic Coast Conference

HISTORY

The year 1907 was a very exciting one for the University of Louisville (U of L). First, from an educational view, the school's liberal arts college was revitalized. Second, U of L began competing in intercollegiate football, basketball, baseball, and track. Six years after having their athletic teams active in intercollegiate competition, Ellen Patterson, the dean's wife, had suggested that the school's athletic board adopt cardinal red and black as the official school colors. At that time, U of L was already using a similar color combination of crimson and black. More than likely, Mrs. Paterson's suggestion of replacing crimson with cardinal was to show U of L's allegiance to the state of Kentucky. You see, the cardinal is Kentucky's state bird. After the board agreed to the color change, U of L teams were soon referred to and eventually nicknamed the Cardinals.

The University of Louisville adopted the cardinal as the school's official mascot after World War II. The cardinal, like the suggested color change, was probably chosen to show the university's loyalty to the state.

SCHOOL NAME: University of Louisiana at Monroe
NICKNAME: Warhawks
MASCOT: hawk ("Ace the Warhawk")
COLORS: maroon and gold
CONFERENCE: Sun Belt Conference

HISTORY

On April 5, 2006, the University of Louisiana at Monroe (ULM) officially changed its nickname from the Indians to the Warhawks. The name change was due to the NCAA having new restrictions against American Indian–themed mascots, which the NCAA now considers to be "hostile and abusive" to American Indians. The Warhawks were chosen in honor of Maj. Gen. Claire Lee Chennault, who was an LSU alumnus who commanded the American Volunteer Group of pilots in the Air Force during World War II. The nickname is synonymous with the aircraft general Chennault and his unit flew, the Curtis P-40 Warhawk.

After ULM officially changed its nickname to the Warhawks, the school's new mascot, Ace the Flying Warhawk, was implemented on June 26, 2006.

ULM's official school colors are maroon and gold. Unfortunately, there is no historical data explaining why those colors were chosen.

SCHOOL NAME:	University of Maryland
NICKNAME:	Terrapins
MASCOT:	terrapin ("Testudo")
COLORS:	red and yellow
CONFERENCE:	Big Ten Conference

HISTORY

Throughout the 1920s, while other intercollegiate schools had intimidating mascots such as tigers, wildcats, and wolves, the University of Maryland was plagued with not having one. So in 1932, Maryland's student newspaper organized a contest in search of an official leader. Dr. H. C. Byrd, the school's football coach who later became the university president, solved this problem by recommending the diamondback (a turtle) as the school's mascot. This idea came to mind because of Mr. Byrd recalling frequent skirmishes he had with these critters as a child growing up near the Chesapeake Bay, in Crisfield, Maryland, where this species of snapping turtle is indigenous. Testudo, the name given to the school mascot, is believed to come from the word "testudines," the scientific classification for turtle.

When the school yearbook, *The Reveille*, changed its name to the *Terrapin* (just a fancy name for a turtle) in 1935, this eventfully became the nickname for all athletic teams at the University of Maryland.

Red and yellow are the colors depicted on the Maryland state flag. For this reason, the University of Maryland also uses the same colors to represent all of its athletic teams.

SCHOOL NAME:	University of Massachusetts–Amherst
NICKNAME:	Minutemen, Minutewomen
MASCOT:	minuteman ("Sam the Minuteman")
COLORS:	black, maroon, and white
CONFERENCE:	Division I FBS Independents

HISTORY

When the University of Massachusetts–Amherst (UMass) (originally named Massachusetts Agricultural College) first started competing in sports, their athletic teams were called the Statesmen, in honor of the roles the statesmen played in the founding of the country. Since the college was an agricultural school, the name Aggies was also used. When the school changed its name to UMass in 1947, the school decided that it was time to for a new nickname. In 1948, in honor of the roles Native Americans played in the history of the commonwealth and for their strength and aggressiveness in defending their lands, Redmen was chosen. However, by the end of the 1972 spring semester, UMass's board of trustees changed the nickname to the Minutemen because of Native Americans in the region believing the Redmen name had derogatory connotations. Minutemen was also chosen because of its ties to the history of the Commonwealth and the instrumental role they played in the early stages of the American Revolution.

Sam the Minuteman is the official mascot for the UMass athletic teams.

The official school colors for UMass athletic teams are black, maroon, and white. Unfortunately, there is no historical data explaining why those colors were chosen.

SCHOOL NAME:	University of Memphis
NICKNAME:	Tigers
MASCOT:	bengal tiger ("Tom")
COLORS:	blue and gray
CONFERENCE:	American Athletic Conference

HISTORY

In 1912, when West Tennessee Normal (formally the University of Memphis) first established a football team to compete in intercollegiate athletics, the school did not have a nickname for its athletic teams. In the final game of the 1914 season, the West Tennessee Normal students had a parade. During this, several students shouted the phrase, "We fight like tigers!" The Tiger name was an instant hit with the student body, but the local newspapers continued to refer to the football team as the Blue and Gray, which was not an official school nickname. However, in 1922, that changed when Coach Lester Barnard had his team come up with a different motto for the students to yell, "Every man a tiger." With that, the Tiger nickname was reborn. However, it was not until 1939 that the University of Memphis made Tigers the official nickname.

In 1972, the University of Memphis's first tiger mascot costume was purchased by the school's booster club (the Highland Hundred) for $1,500. Then on November 11 of that same year, the tiger was introduced to the university. A contest was then held to decide on a nickname. More than 2,500 entries were submitted to a committee, which was chaired by Judge Harry Pierotti. A few of the more popular names submitted were Spook, Sampson, Goliath, Bengo, Sultan, Sahib, Big Cat, Ptah, Touchdown, Sonny, Tom, and Shiloh. Eventually, the list was narrowed down to two final names, Tom and Shane. At the conclusion of the contest, Tom was chosen as the official nickname of the school's mascot.

In the early 1900s, the student body chose royal blue and gray as the official school colors for the University of Memphis. Those colors were chosen to represent the unity of the north and south in a nation that was still recovering from the effects of the Civil War.

SCHOOL NAME:	University of Miami
NICKNAME:	Hurricanes
MASCOT:	ibis ("Sebastian")
COLORS:	orange, green, and white
CONFERENCE:	Atlantic Coast Conference

HISTORY

The history behind how the University of Miami derived its official nickname is one of controversy. One story has it that in 1927, the Miami football team held a meeting to select a nickname. They chose Hurricanes, hoping their team would wipe out opponents just as the devastating storm did on September 16, 1926. Another version holds that when Porter Norris, a tight end on the 1926 football team, was asked, "What should the team be called?" Jake Bell, a *Miami News* columnist, said, "Hurricanes," since the opening game had been postponed by one.

The ibis was chosen as the official mascot for the University of Miami because of its survival instincts, as it is the last sign of wildlife before a hurricane and the first to reappear after the storm has passed. The mascot goes by the name of Sebastian because San Sebastian Hall (a resident hall on campus) was the sight of the first ibis mascot tryouts in 1957.

The official school colors for the University of Miami's athletic teams are orange, green, and white. Those colors were selected in 1926 and represent the Florida orange tree (orange), the orange tree's leaves (green), and its blossoms (white).

SCHOOL NAME:	University of Michigan
NICKNAME:	Wolverines
MASCOT:	wolverine
COLORS:	maize and blue
CONFERENCE:	Big Ten Conference

HISTORY

When trying to determine why the University of Michigan selected the wolverine as its official mascot, it can be found that there is no known reason this particular animal was chosen. However, there are several theories.

The first theory had to do with the trading of animal pelts in Sault Station Marie, Michigan. This was a major exchange station for American Indians, trappers, and fur traders, who would exchange goods and eventually ship their products off to the Eastern United States. Because many of the more popular furs shipped were, in fact, wolverine pelts, the traders may have referred to them as Michigan Wolverines, leading to the state nickname and ultimately to the University of Michigan representation.

The second theory involved the large population of French settlers who moved to Michigan in the late 1700s. Since other settlers judged the French as having gluttonous or "wolverine-like" appetites, this could explain why they were called Wolverines.

The last theory has to do with an 1803 state border dispute between Michigan and Ohio. While both states were trying to determine where the state line should be drawn, Michiganders were called Wolverines. However, this theory does not specify whether the Michigan natives coined this name themselves to show their determination and strength, or if the Ohioans dubbed the name because of the gluttonous habit of the wolverine. From then on, Michigan was called the Wolverine State, and after the University of Michigan was founded in 1817, it decided to recognize the university's official nickname and mascot in honor of the state it represented.

When the University of Michigan recognized the importance of its institution in claiming an official school color, a committee from the literary department chose the colors maize and blue on February 12, 1867.

SCHOOL NAME:	University of Minnesota
NICKNAME:	Golden Gophers
MASCOT:	gopher ("Goldy Gopher")
COLORS:	maroon and gold
CONFERENCE:	Big Ten Conference

HISTORY

Minnesota became a state in 1857and was nicknamed the Gopher State, after a very disrespectful cartoon was published showing nine gophers with the heads of local politicians pulling a locomotive. Apparently, there was a legislative proposal to build a $5 million railroad in western Minnesota, and this did not fare well with a lot of people. Overtime, the university decided to use the gopher nickname and mascot.

In 1880, the University of Minnesota was preparing for its annual spring graduation, and for the last twenty-nine years, different colors were always used for graduation ribbons and other occasions. By this time, the school's president had decided to start a tradition of using the same colors for all events. He asked English instructor, Mrs. Augusta Smith, to decide on those colors. She chose maroon and gold, which was a big hit with students and faculty. Eventually, maroon and gold became the official school colors.

SCHOOL NAME:	University of Mississippi
NICKNAME:	Rebels
MASCOT:	shark ("Landshark Tony")
COLORS:	red and blue
CONFERENCE:	Southeastern Conference

HISTORY

The official nickname for the University of Mississippi's (Ole Miss) athletic teams is the Rebels. A judge from Vicksburg, Mississippi, named Ben Guider takes the credit for the Rebel nickname. This story first emerged when the *Mississippian*, Ole Miss's school newspaper, decided to sponsor a contest to select a nickname for the university. In doing so, the newspaper decided to contact as many sportswriters as possible for suggestions once they received the final list of the proposed nicknames. Rebels was one of five entries selected from a list of more than two hundred names. Of the forty-two sportswriters contacted, twenty-one responded. Moreover, eighteen of them suggested the Rebels. When the university athletic committee heard the results, committee chairman Judge William Hemingway said, "If eighteen writers wish to use Rebels, I shall not rebel, so let it go, Ole Miss Rebels."

Two years later, Colonel Reb made his debut to Ole Miss students as the leading illustration on the Ole Miss's yearbook. Colonel Reb has become a near official university insignia and mascot for Ole Miss. In 2010, Ole Miss's administration decided that it was now time to replace Colonel Reb, because it was inappropriate to have a mascot that symbolized the Confederacy and slavery. So a competition was held, and the three finalists were the Landshark, Rebel the Black Bear, and Hotty Toddy. At the conclusion of the event, Rebel the Black Bear was the winner. That mascot was chosen because the animal was based on the short story "The Bear" by William Faulkner, who was an Ole Miss alumni. Rebel the Bear served as the school's mascot for the next seven years. Students were unhappy with their selection because a bear had no attachment to Ole Miss, but in "The

Bear" short story, the bear is killed. As a result, his presence became very uninspiring. So in 2017, another contest was held involving the same three finalists from 2010. This time, the Landshark was declared the winner. Consequently, in 2018, Landshark Tony was unveiled as Ole Miss's new official mascot. The mascot's name is associated with the late Tony Fein, who was a former Ole Miss linebacker who created the Fins Up celebration tradition, which ultimately inspired the mascot. At the conclusion of big plays, defensive players (Landshark Defense) form their hands on their helmets in the shape of a shark fin.

Prior to Ole Miss's first football team competing in intercollegiate athletic competition in 1893, the players pondered over which colors should be used to represent their football team. Following the team's in-depth discussion on possible adopted colors, the team manager suggested that, in addition to the Ole Miss's football team already exemplifying the team spirit of Harvard and Yale, they should adopt their school colors as well. With that said, the crimson of Harvard and the blue of Yale became the official football team colors and, in time, the official school colors of Ole Miss.

SCHOOL NAME:	University of Missouri
NICKNAME:	Tigers
MASCOT:	tiger ("Truman")
COLORS:	black and yellow
CONFERENCE:	Southeastern Conference

HISTORY

Around 1890, the tiger was chosen by the University of Missouri to represent the school's athletic teams and mascot in honor of a brave Columbia militia group who defended the school from possible attacks by pro-Confederate guerrillas toward the end of the Civil War. In doing so, the group took the nickname of Tigers.

Truman, the University of Missouri mascot, was named in honor of Pres. Harry S. Truman, who is a Missouri native.

Black and yellow were selected as the official colors for the University of Missouri because this color combination represents the color of a tiger.

SCHOOL NAME:	University of Nebraska
NICKNAME:	Cornhuskers
MASCOT:	"Herbie Husker", "Lil' Red"
COLORS:	scarlet and cream
CONFERENCE:	Big Ten Conference

HISTORY

Prior to the 1900s, the University of Nebraska (UN) football teams were referred to as the Old Gold Knight, Antelopes, Rattlesnake Boys, and, eventually, the Bugeaters, because of the numerous bullbats that inhabit the state and feed on bugs. However, after UN had its first losing season in a decade, the football team had decided to go in a different direction. Charles S. (Cy) Sherman, who was the sportswriter for the *Lincoln Star,* concurred with the football team's decision and also felt it was now time to come up with a better name than the Bugeaters. Mr. Sherman liked the name Cornhusker, which at the time was the nickname for the University of Iowa football team. In 1900, Mr. Sherman started referring to the UN football team as the Cornhuskers when Iowa fans started calling its football team the Hawkeyes. The name was an instant success and became the official nickname for UN sports teams. In 1945, Cornhusker became the official nickname for the state of Nebraska. UN and the state chose that name because husking corn was done by hand by early settlers before the invention of husking machinery. The name also refers to natives or residents that live in the state of Nebraska.

From 1955 to 1974, there were several name changes made to UN's unofficial mascot. These included Corncob Man, Husky Husker, Mr. Cornhead, Harry Husker, and Herbie Husker and were created by cartoonist Dirk West and became UN's official school mascot in 1974. Then in 1984, Lil' Red arrived and became the school's second official mascot.

The official school colors for UN's athletic teams are scarlet and cream. Unfortunately, there is no historical data explaining why those colors were chosen.

SCHOOL NAME:	University of Nevada at Las Vegas
NICKNAME:	Rebels
MASCOT:	rebel ("Hey Reb")
COLORS:	scarlet and gray
CONFERENCE:	Mountain West Conference

HISTORY

When the University of Nevada at Las Vegas (UNLV) came into existence, it felt the need to compete with the University of Nevada at Reno, since it was now the second college under the University of Nevada higher education system. Moreover, with Nevada Reno being located in northern Nevada and having a wolf as a mascot, UNLV, which is located in southern Nevada, chose Beauregard, a wolf with Confederate Army characteristics, as its official school mascot. To add, since UNLV was, in fact, rebelling against Nevada Reno, the school chose Rebels as their nickname. However, in 1970, after a group of black athletes voiced their disapproval of playing for a college whose mascot represented negative connotations toward African Americans, UNLV officials changed its mascot to Hey Reb, UNLV's new rebel against Nevada Reno.

Since UNLV once had a mascot with Confederate Army characteristics, the Confederate Army colors of scarlet and gray were chosen as UNLV's official school colors.

SCHOOL NAME:	University of Nevada at Reno
NICKNAME:	Wolf Pack
MASCOT:	wolf ("Alphie", "Wolfie Jr." and "Luna")
COLORS:	silver and blue
CONFERENCE:	Mountain West Conference

HISTORY

In the 1928–29 student handbook, the University of Nevada at Reno (UNR) started calling all of its athletic teams the Wolf Pack. This name was chosen for a couple of reasons. First, people who reside in Reno and the surrounding area are very familiar with wolves because that animal makes its home in the surrounding Sierra Nevada Mountains. Second, during the 1921–22 athletic season, a local sportswriter referred to the highly spirited football team as "a pack of wolves." The name stuck, and soon, all UNR athletic teams were being called the Wolves. Last, since all athletic teams consist of a group of players, the word "pack" followed quickly.

In the 1921–22 athletic season, UNR sports teams were known as the Wolves. Then in 1923, the wolf became the school's official mascot. Years later, Wolfie made his debut. Then in 1999, Alphie took over the cheering duties from his father, Wolfie. In 2007, Wolfie Jr. joined his older brother, Alphie. Then in 2013, the wolf pack was finally made complete when Luna, who is the sister to Alphie and Wolfie Jr., made her debut.

UNR chose blue and silver as their official school colors because they are also the colors of the Nevada state flag. Blue represents the color of Lake Tahoe and the mountain bluebird, Nevada's state bird, and silver represents the color of Nevada's state mineral.

SCHOOL NAME:	University of New Mexico
NICKNAME:	Lobos
MASCOT:	lobo ("Lobo Louis" and "Lobo Lucy")
COLORS:	cherry and silver
CONFERENCE:	Mountain West Conference

HISTORY

In 1892, when the University of New Mexico (UNM) first started playing football, the team was strictly known as the Boy or Varsities. Those names were chosen to differentiate themselves from prep school kids. In 1917, UNM's student body decided to take a serious approach to deciding on a new name for the school newspaper, which was simply called the *University of New Mexico Weekly*, and a mascot. Some of the names that were suggested included the Rattler, the Sand Devil, the Ki-yo-te, and the Cherry and Silver. None of those names were a hit with the students. For the next three years, UNM was still without a mascot, and the school newspaper name had not changed. On September 22, 1922, a student council meeting was held to determine a mascot name for UNM. During that time, many colleges that were competing in athletics were using mascots to represent their teams. George S. Bryant, who was the editor of the *UNM Weekly* and the manager of the football team, suggested the name Lobo, which is the Spanish word for wolf. The lobo, Bryant said, is respected for being cunning, feared for his prowess, and is the leader of the pack. This was the ideal name to represent the characteristics of UNM's football team. The name was enthusiastically accepted by the council, and consequently, Lobo became the official nickname and mascot for UNM athletic teams. Also, the school newspaper name was changed to the *New Mexico Daily Lobo.*

In the 1920s, a live wolf was used to represent UNM athletic teams. But when a child was bitten by the wolf while being teased, the school decided to do away with a live animal and have it replaced with a costumed human mascot. Lobo Louis made his debut in the 1960s, and Lobo Lucy arrived in the 1980s.

In the early 1890s, UNM's school colors were black and gold. Ms. Harriet Janness, who was a faculty member at the university, suggested that those colors be changed to crimson and silver because they did not give a true feeling to New Mexico. Crimson would symbolize the evening glow of the majestic Sandia Mountains to the east. Silver represented the Rio Grande, which looked like a silver ribbon winding through the valley below. Those color changes were approved by the faculty, but crimson was eventually changed to cherry, which represented the color of the Sandia sunset. From 1973 to 1979, the official colors of UNM's athletic teams were turquoise. But in 1980, cherry and silver once again became UNM's official athletic team colors.

SCHOOL NAME:	University of North Carolina–Chapel Hill
NICKNAME:	Tar Heels
MASCOT:	ram ("Rameses")
COLORS:	Carolina blue and white
CONFERENCE:	Atlantic Coast Conference

HISTORY

Besides the name Tar Heel being the nickname for the University of North Carolina (UNC), it is the state's nickname as well. The origin of this name is the state's abundance of naval stores, which extracted and produced tar, pitch, and turpentine from the state's pine tree forests. Although there are multiple stories that suggest how the name came about, the story that involves the Revolutionary War seems to carry the most credibility.

Story has it that the name was derived when Lord Cornwallis's troops forded through North Carolina's Tar River with tar on their feet as they emerged on the other side, leaving a trail of tar heel footprints en route to Yorktown, New York.

Many people have always asked the question, "If UNC is known as the Tar Heels, why do they have a ram as a mascot?" Well, to answer that question, one would have to go back to the 1920s, when UNC had no mascot. Back then, Carolina students were eager for one, especially since school rivals Georgia and North Carolina State had a bulldog and a wolf. This all changed in 1922, when Jack Merrit, a UNC bruising fullback, who was known as "the Battering Ram" for the way he stormed through the oppositions defensive lines, led Carolina to a 9–1 record.

"Carolina blue" and white were chosen as the school colors for the University of North Carolina because the blue represents Dialectic Literary Society (emblem of steadfastness and truth) and white being the color of Philanthropic Literary Society.

SCHOOL NAME:	University of North Carolina–Charlotte
NICKNAME:	49ers
MASCOT:	miner ("Norm the Miner")
COLORS:	green and white
CONFERENCE:	Conference USA

HISTORY

The official nickname for the University of North Carolina–Charlotte (UNC Charlotte) athletic teams is the 49ers. That name was chosen because, in 1949, Bonnie Cone and her supporters convinced North Carolina Legislature, that Charlotte needed a permanent college for higher learning as an alternative to UNC Charlotte, which at the time was an off-campus center for the University of North Carolina–Chapel Hill. As a result, Charlotte College was established that year.

A miner was chosen as UNC Charlotte's official mascot as a tribute to the Reed Gold Mine, which was located in nearby Concord and, in 1799, was the site of the United States first gold find. An on-campus contest was conducted to name the mascot, and through popular student body vote, the name Norm was selected.

When UNC Charlotte became a part of the UNC system, the university wanted their colors to be different and unique from the other three colleges (UNC–Chapel Hill, UNC–Greensboro, and North Carolina State University) in the area. When a committee was formed, the members realized that white was a common color at the other three schools, so green was selected. This is because it was unique to Charlotte College and distinct from blue at Chapel Hill, gold at Greensboro, and red at NC State.

SCHOOL NAME:	University of North Texas
NICKNAME:	Mean Green
MASCOT:	eagle ("Scrappy")
COLORS:	green and white
CONFERENCE:	Conference USA

HISTORY

The University of North Texas (UNT) nickname has been the Mean Green since 1966, because of their football team having such a fierce defense. Two outstanding defensive players were a part of that team and went on to play in the NFL, Joe Greene and Cedric Hardman. Moreover, there are two different stories that explain how the UNT nickname was derived. The first version had to do with Sidney Sue Graham, who was the wife of UNT's sports information director, shouting out, "That's the way, Mean Greene!" in response to Greene making a tackle. The second version was that Ms. Graham shouted out, "That's the way, Mean Green!" because of the team's defense. Regardless which version is true, Ms. Graham's husband started using the nickname for UNT team press releases, and the name caught on with the media.

In 1922, students voted to make an eagle the official mascot for UNT teams instead of a lion or a dragon. On October 6, 1950, the first live eagle appeared at the UNT versus Southwestern Oklahoma game. The eagle was named Scrappy. In 1969, UNT decided to start using a costumed eagle mascot instead of a live eagle. In 1974, UNT thought the name Scrappy was too warlike and changed the name to Eppy. However, in 1995, the mascot name was changed back the Scrappy, and that name has been used ever since.

In 1902, green and white were selected to be the official school colors for UNT sports teams. Rumor has it that those colors were chosen when someone stated, "Mother Nature would be kind to those using her colors."

SCHOOL NAME:	University of Notre Dame
NICKNAME:	Fighting Irish
MASCOT:	leprechaun
COLORS:	blue and gold
CONFERENCE:	Division I FBS Independents

HISTORY

When discussing the history of University of Notre Dame (Notre Dame) football, many different stories surface about when the term "Fighting Irish" came about and who can take credit for first using it. However, the University of Notre Dame nickname origin is quite obvious.

Large amounts of Irish prizefighting boxers in the nineteenth century were associated with students, faculty, and administrators. Therefore, choice for a nickname was not very difficult. However, even though there are recorded facts that indicate that the Fighting Irish nickname has been used as far back as 1889, it was used interchangeably with a slew of other names. Hence, it wasn't until 1925 that the Fighting Irish nickname became popularized. Moreover, the man responsible for this happening was a sportswriter named Frances Wallace.

After being hired by Knute Rockne as a student press agent for the football team in 1920, Wallace continued to use the Fighting Irish nickname and variations of it as well. After graduating in 1923 and becoming a sportswriter in New York, he noticed that some of the other local city papers started referring to the Notre Dame football team as the Rambling Irish, Wandering Irish, Rockne's Ramblers, and Rockne's Rovers. All of which signify that the school was a "football factory" and that their players were always on the road and never in class. Needless to say, this did not fare well with Wallace (now a Notre Dame alumnus) or the University of Notre Dame administration. The Notre Dame administration detested these nicknames and wanted to discourage them.

To help support the administrations reactions, Wallace tried to come up with an alternative nonethnic and nonnomadic nickname. The result was the Blue Comets, which was based on the team's blue uniforms and quick offense. However, the likeness of this name never did catch on with football fans. So when Wallace started working for the *New York Post* in 1925, he once again used the Fighting Irish nickname. This, of course, set the tone for other newspaper sportswriters as well.

When Wallace started working for the *New York Daily News,* his writing and use of the "Fighting Irish" term was now exposed to a much larger audience. The wire services also started utilizing the term. Thus, when the editor of the *World* wrote to Notre Dame's newspaper, the *Golden Dome,* asking the administration what their position was in regard to the Fighting Irish nickname, President Walsh responded by giving all publications his approval to use the Fighting Irish nickname.

To closely associate with the Fighting Irish nickname, Notre Dame's official mascot is a leprechaun, which is supposed to bring magical power and good luck to the teams. However, the leprechaun was not always the mascot. For many years, Notre Dame used Irish terrier dogs. The first was Brick, who made his debut at the Notre Dame versus Pennsylvania football game on November 8, 1930. The leprechaun became Notre Dame's official mascot in 1965.

Although at this point in time there is no conclusive documentation to support this fact, it is believed that the Notre Dame's school colors came from the direct correlation of the golden statue of the Virgin Mary atop the Main Building reflecting a striking image off the blue summer sky.

SCHOOL NAME:	University of Oklahoma
NICKNAME:	Sooners
MASCOT:	covered wagon ("the Sooner Schooner")
COLORS:	crimson and cream
CONFERENCE:	Big 12 Conference

HISTORY

Why are University of Oklahoma sports teams called the Sooners? Well, to get the answer to that question, you would have to go back to 1889. Back then, settlers from around the world were going out west to the prairies to start new lives by staking their claim on getting free land. However, to achieve that, the Oklahoma Territory required these settlers to partake in the Land Run. One of the rules of the Land Run was that all participants searching for free land lots had to start at the same time. This was enforced by firing a cannon. All settlers that started at that time were called Boomers. If you started too soon, you were called a Sooner. In 1908, the Sooner nickname was derived from a university pep club called the Sooner Rooters.

The Sooner Schooner, which is a covered wagon powered by two ponies named Boomer and Sooner, was chosen as the official school mascot in 1980, because of it being the type of transportation that was used back in the 1800s by pioneers wanting to settle in Oklahoma.

In 1895, Ms. May Overstreet, who was the only female faculty member at the University of Oklahoma, was asked to chair a committee to determine the university's official school colors. The committee selected crimson and cream, and they were approved with great enthusiasm by the student body.

SCHOOL NAME:	University of Oregon
NICKNAME:	Ducks
MASCOT:	duck ("Puddles")
COLORS:	yellow and green
CONFERENCE:	Pacific 12 Conference

HISTORY

The history behind the University of Oregon (UO) nickname stems all the way back to the 1800s. During that time, Oregonians (people from Oregon) and western Oregonian miners were called Webfoots, Webfeet, or Webfooters by Californian minors, because the weather in western Oregon was always rainy and muddy. So in 1926, the editor of the school's newspaper started calling Oregon sports teams the Webfoots (the Webfooted Ducks), which became the official nickname. However, sportswriters started referring to UO teams as simply the Ducks. After decades of the Duck name being used to reference UO sports teams, in 1978, Ducks became the official nickname for the University of Oregon.

From the early 1920s through the early 1940s, Oregon used a real duck named Puddles as its mascot. Eventually, the university decided to use a costumed version of the mascot instead of a live animal.

In 1893, lemon yellow and emerald green were chosen as UO's official school colors. The colors are found in the state flower, which is the Oregon grape. The yellow is from the blossom of the flower, and the color green is from the leaf.

SCHOOL NAME:	University of Pittsburgh
NICKNAME:	Panthers
MASCOT:	panther ("Roc")
COLORS:	blue and gold
CONFERENCE:	Atlantic Coast Conference

HISTORY

In the fall of 1909, a meeting was set up between alumni and students at the University of Pittsburgh (Pitt) for the sole purpose of selecting a nickname to represent its athletic teams. At the conclusion of that meeting, Panthers was the selected choice. The person who made that suggestion was a gentleman by the name of Paul P.M. Baird. Panthers was chosen for a number of reasons. First, the panther is a formidable animal that was indigenous to the Pittsburgh region. Second, it has ancient heraldic standing as a noble animal. Third, it was the happy accident of alliteration. Fourth, the color of the panther's fur is very close to one of Pitt's official school colors, which is gold. Last, at that time, no other school competing in college athletics had that nickname.

The official mascot for Pitt is a panther. The panther has been a representative for Pitt athletic teams since 1909. The name of Pitt's costumed mascot is Roc. That name was given to him sometime in the 1990s, in honor of former Pitt football player Steve Petro, who was nicknamed the Rock in his playing days.

The official school colors for Pitt athletic teams are blue and gold. Those colors were selected sometime during the 1880s by a student body committee led by William Johnston, who served on the student newspaper and was valedictorian of his class.

SCHOOL NAME: University of South Alabama
NICKNAME: Jaguars
MASCOT: jaguar ("South Paw", "Miss Pawla")
COLORS: red, white, and blue
CONFERENCE: Sun Belt Conference

HISTORY

The official nickname for the University of South Alabama's (USA) athletic teams is the Jaguars. That name was selected by the school's board of trustees in 1965.

In 1968, a USA student by the name of Toxie Craft donated a year-old South American jaguar to the school after hearing that USA's Jaguar Club was trying to acquire one to be the school's mascot. In 1969, a contest was held to name the mascot, and the name Mischka was selected from a list of students, faculty, and staff submissions. Student Bob Kirsch submitted the winning name, which is Russian for Michael. Kirsch got his idea from Mischka, who is a dancing bear associated with the Russian circus. However, for legal concerns, USA decided to discontinue using a live animal as a mascot after Mischka was seen wandering around campus when her cage was mistakenly left unlocked. In 1971, USA started using costumed jaguar mascots in place of a live animal. Student Donnie Butler was USA's first mascot. In the late 1970s, a Name the Mascot contest was held, and the name South Paw was chosen. In 1992, Miss Pawla joined South Paw.

On March 31, 1965, USA's official school colors of black and gold were accepted by the board of trustees. Those colors were chosen by a vote of the student body. However, when it was discovered by USA's first athletic director, Dr. Mel Lucus, that nearby Davidson High School had the same colors, the next year, the coaches decided to change the colors to red, white, and blue to go along with USA. Consequently, another student body vote was conducted, and they became USA's official school colors.

SCHOOL NAME:	University of South Carolina
NICKNAME:	Gamecocks
MASCOT:	gamecock ("Cocky")
COLORS:	garnet and black
CONFERENCE:	Southeastern Conference

HISTORY

When the topic of college nicknames comes up in conversation, it's known that, without a doubt, the University of South Carolina (USC) is the only school in the nation that uses Gamecocks as its official nickname and mascot, a tradition that goes back more than ninety-five years. However, prior to that time, USC's athletic teams were known as the Game Cocks. It wasn't until 1903 when the *State*, Columbia's morning newspaper, shortened the name to one word, and USC elected to change its official nickname to the Gamecocks. This nickname was chosen because of the feisty and spirited attitude displayed by USC's early football teams.

A gamecock, of course, is a fighting rooster that was used for cockfighting, which was a popular sport throughout the United States in the nineteenth century. A cockfight would last until the death of one of the roosters was established. For humanitarian reasons, cockfighting is banned in most states but is still held illegally in many areas. The state of South Carolina was one of the more popular areas that was closely connected with the breeding and training of fighting gamecocks. For this reason, USC's mascot is also a gamecock and goes by the name of Cocky.

Garnet and black were chosen as the official colors for USC because these colors are synonymous to the plumage of the gamecock.

SCHOOL NAME: University of South Florida
NICKNAME: Bulls
MASCOT: bull ("Rocky the Bull")
COLORS: green and gold
CONFERENCE: American Athletic Conference

HISTORY

Not too long after the inception of the University of South Florida (USF) in 1956, a contest was held to determine the official nickname and mascot for the university's athletic teams. The finalists were the Golden Brahman Bulls, the Olympians, the Cougars, the Buccaneers, and the Golden Eagles. At the conclusion of that contest, the Golden Brahman Bulls was the winner. That name was chosen because of Florida's state history in cattle raising.

On November 17, 1962, the Golden Brahman Bull made its debut as USF's official mascot. In the early 1980s, USF's nickname was shortened to the Bulls. Then at the start of the 2004 football season, Rocky the Bull was introduced as USF's new mascot.

The official school colors for USF athletic teams are green and gold. Unfortunately, there is no historical data explaining why those colors were chosen.

SCHOOL NAME:	University of Southern California
NICKNAME:	Trojans
MASCOT:	horse ("Traveler")
COLORS:	cardinal red and gold
CONFERENCE:	Pacific 12 Conference

HISTORY

When the University of Southern California (USC) first started competing in intercollegiate athletics, the school's athletic teams were nicknamed the Methodists or Wesleyans. Warren Bovard, the athletic director of USC and the son of university president Dr. George Bovard, decided to seek a new school name for USC after university officials voiced their dislike of the current names. In doing so, he decided to ask Owen Bird, the sports editor for the *Los Angeles Times*, to select an appropriate nickname. You see, at this time, both university officials and Bird knew that many of the opponents that the USC athletic teams were competing against were bigger, stronger, and more talented than their athletes. However, Bird could not help but notice the tremendous fighting spirit and dedication of the USC teams. This, in turn, gave him the idea to nickname all USC teams the Trojans because, to Bird, Trojans were men who would fight to the end and would strive to perform to the best of their ability regardless of the conditions, odds, or situation. Bird first used the Trojan nickname in a sports article prior to a showdown between USC and Stanford in 1912. As a result, the name stuck, and Trojans became the new official nickname for USC

Traveler, USC's white horse mascot, has appeared at USC games for nearly forty years. He made his first debut in 1961 when special events director Bob Jani persuaded Saukko, the USC Trojan, to ride his white horse around the coliseum during USC games. From that time on, every time USC scores, the band plays "Conquest," and Traveler gallops around the coliseum. However, Traveler was not the first white horse to appear at USC sporting events. The first horse appeared at a 1927 USC football game, when rider Louis Shields signed a four-year contract to ride a horse owned by a local banker.

Prior to 1895, the official school color for USC was gold, and the color for the College of Liberal Arts was cardinal red. At that time, all academic departments at USC had their own colors, and since the College of Liberal Arts was the largest academic unit, it too had its own color. However, in 1895, USC officials chose to use both colors to represent USC and their athletic teams.

SCHOOL NAME:	University of Southern Mississippi
NICKNAME:	Golden Eagles
MASCOT:	golden eagle ("Seymour d' Campus")
COLORS:	black and gold
CONFERENCE:	Conference USA

HISTORY

After being known as the Southerners for many years, University of Southern Mississippi athletic teams underwent an identity change on November 11, 1972. More than four hundred different suggestions were made during the five-month campaign to determine a new nickname. Suggestions were turned in to an ad hoc committee of alumni, students, and friends of the university. The committee narrowed the suggestions down to five possible nicknames, all of which appeared on a ballot. The committee, along with faculty and staff members, voted on the five finalists: (Golden Eagles, Golden Raiders, Southerners, Timber Wolves, and War Lords). It took two votes to get the 60 percent majority needed, but Golden Eagles eventually won over Southerners.

Seymour was chosen as the name of the costumed golden eagle mascot. His full name is Seymour d' Campus. The name was inspired by Seymour d' Fair, who was the 1984 World's Fair mascot and portrayed by Jeff Davis, who was Southern Mississippi's former 1983 mascot.

Prior to a woman by the name of Moran Pope attending Mississippi Normal College (the former name of the University of Southern Mississippi), Mrs. Pope attended Carson High School in 1911. While at Carson, members of her senior class argued about the selection of class colors. While on a class trip, Mrs. Pope saw a vast amount of black-eyed Susan flowers in a pine field. Mrs. Pope found the black-and-gold flowers to be fascinating and asked some of the students to gather up a bunch of the flowers and bring them back to Carson. She then suggested that black and gold be the senior class colors. Mrs. Pope's suggestion won. Soon after Mississippi Normal

College opened in 1912, Mrs. Pope attended high school and college. Mr. Cook, who was the school's president, asked that a committee form to determine Mississippi Normal College school colors. Mrs. Pope was selected as one of the five members of that committee. When Mrs. Pope suggested black and gold, those two colors were submitted to the student body by the committee for approval. Black and gold were eventually chosen as the official school colors for Mississippi Normal College.

SCHOOL NAME: University of Tennessee
NICKNAME: Volunteers
MASCOT: bluetick coonhound ("Smokey")
COLORS: orange and white
CONFERENCE: Southeastern Conference

HISTORY

The University of Tennessee chose to nickname its athletic teams the Volunteers because Tennessee is known as the Volunteer State. Tennessee acquired this nickname when Gov. Aaron V. Brown called on 2,800 men to fight in the Mexican War. In the end, a total of thirty thousand men volunteered, so the term "Volunteer State" is used to recognize that Tennesseans will go above and beyond the call of duty when their country needs them.

In 1953, a student pep club took a poll that asked Tennessee students to come up with a mascot that would represent its athletic teams. A coonhound, which is a native breed of Tennessee, was the chosen mascot. Now, a name needed to be selected. A contest was held during halftime of a Mississippi State game, and the late reverend Bill Brooks entered his prizewinning dog, Brooks Blue Smokey, along with other bluetick coonhounds, to decide a winner. Each dog was introduced over the loud speaker, followed by cheers from the crowd. When Brooks Blue Smokey name was called, the crowd cheered the loudest. Consequently, Smokey the Bluetick Coonhound became the official mascot for the University of Tennessee.

In 1891, Charles Moore, who was a member of Tennessee's first football team, chose orange and white as the schools colors. Those colors were later approved by the student body. Mr. Moore chose those colors because they are the same colors of the common American daisy, which grows on top of The Hill. The Hill is a part of the university's campus that is situated on a rising bank above the north shore of the Tennessee River. The Hill is where the University of Tennessee (formally named Blount College) was first established.

SCHOOL NAME:	University of Texas
NICKNAME:	Longhorns
MASCOT:	longhorn steer ("Bevo")
COLORS:	burnt orange and white
CONFERENCE:	Big 12 Conference

HISTORY

With the vast amount of privately owned land occupied by ranches in the state of Texas, it's no wonder that the longhorn steer is such a common animal to see in the country's third-largest state. More than likely, this is what prompted the University of Texas (UT) to choose the Longhorn as its official nickname. In 1916, 126 UT alumni decided to show their school pride by purchasing the school's first mascot by each contributing one dollar. A few years later, the UT mascot was stolen by some Texas A&M students after a football game between the two schools. They branded "13–0" (the score of the previous year's Texas versus Texas A&M football game) on the steer. To save face, UT students got creative and managed to change "13–0" to "Bevo," which was the name of a popular local beer. As a result, Bevo became the name of UT's mascot.

In 1900, the UT student body opted to go with orange and white instead of orange and maroon as the official colors. This final decision won by thirteen votes. In 1928, the orange color was altered to a dark burnt orange after UT football coach Clyde Littlefield discovered that the jerseys being used at that time had the tendency to fade when washed in hot water. With the onset of World War II, the football jerseys went back to a lighter orange because of the shortage of dye. Then in 1962, the burnt orange color was used once again, this time by Coach Darrell Royal. The board of regents went with burnt orange and white as their final decision.

SCHOOL NAME:	University of Texas at El Paso
NICKNAME:	Miners
MASCOT:	miner ("Paydirt Pete")
COLORS:	orange, white, and blue
CONFERENCE:	Conference USA

HISTORY

In 1967, the University of Texas at El Paso (UTEP) took its present name. However, in 1913, the school was called the State School of Mines and Metallurgy. Moreover, because there is no factual documentation, rumor has it that UTEP's official Miner nickname was derived from the school's original name.

In their effort to represent the Miner nickname with a credible mascot, it took UTEP four attempts before they got it right. The first two were burros named Clyde and Henry, respectively. Both were not very popular with students and fans alike. Then in 1980, Sweet Pete arrived. Sweet Pete was a lovable little animated miner that, in time, also became unpopular with fans because of his lack of portrayed toughness. In 1999, Paydirt Pete, who was another animated miner, came on to the scene and was immediately accepted by UTEP fans because of his mean demeanor.

Although it cannot be determined why UTEP chose orange and white to represent its athletic teams, sometime in the 1980s, students voted to add blue as an additional color. Consequently, orange, white, and blue became the official school colors for UTEP's athletic teams.

SCHOOL NAME: University of Texas at San Antonio
NICKNAME: Roadrunners
MASCOT: roadrunner ("Rowdy")
COLORS: white, orange, and blue
CONFERENCE: Conference USA

HISTORY

The official nickname and mascot for the University of Texas at San Antonio (UTSA) athletic teams is the Roadrunners. That name was chosen back in 1977, when the Student Representative Assembly had an open debate to select a nickname. When Roadrunners was selected instead of Armadillos in a very close student election, a bonfire celebration was held later on that year announcing UTSA's official nickname and mascot. Rowdy is the name of UTSA's mascot, and he made his debut on March 1, 2008, at a homecoming basketball game against Texas A&M University–Corpus Christi.

The official school colors for UTSA's athletic teams are white, orange, and blue. In 1975, blue was selected as the third color by student leaders and UTSA's administration.

SCHOOL NAME: University of Toledo
NICKNAME: Rockets
MASCOT: "Rocky the Rocket"
COLORS: blue and gold
CONFERENCE: Mid-American Conference

HISTORY

In 1923, the University of Toledo (UT) played a football game in Pittsburgh against heavily favored Carnegie Tech. During that game, sportswriters realized that UT did not have a nickname, so they pressed James Neal, who was a UT student working in the press box, to come up with a nickname. Although UT was the underdog and ended up losing the game 32–12, James was impressed with their flashy performance where they were able to recover several embarrassing fumbles from Tech. Consequently, he thought Skyrockets would be a good nickname for UT. Over time, sportswriters shortened the name to Rockets, which eventually became the official nickname for UT sports teams.

UT's official mascot, Rocky the Rocket, was created in the 1966–67 academic year by a student government organization called the Spirits and Traditions Committee.

On December 1, 1919, the Varsity T Club, which was an organization made up of fourteen athletes, selected midnight blue and gold as the official school colors for UT.

SCHOOL NAME:	University of Tulsa
NICKNAME:	Golden Hurricane
MASCOT:	"Captain Cane"
COLORS:	royal blue, old gold, and crimson
CONFERENCE:	American Athletic Conference

HISTORY

The nickname for University of Tulsa (TU) athletic teams is the Golden Hurricanes. The name was chosen in 1922 by TU's head football coach H. M. Archer. He got the idea from the gold and black football team uniforms and also because of a remark that was made during practice. Someone described the team as "roaring through opponents" during their undefeated season, which included big wins over Texas A&M and the University of Arkansas. Initially, Coach Archer wanted the nickname to be the Golden Tornados, but at that time, that was the name of Georgia Tech's athletic teams. Therefore, Coach Archer decided to substitute the name "hurricane" for "tornado" and had his football team vote on the name prior to them playing Texas A&M. The team voted in favor of hurricane, thus making the Golden Hurricanes TU's official nickname.

Captain Cane has been TU's official mascot since 1994. He is a superhero that has the power to summon weather.

TU's official school colors are royal blue, old gold, and crimson. Unfortunately, there is no historical data explaining why those colors were chosen.

SCHOOL NAME:	University of Utah
NICKNAME:	Utes
MASCOT:	red-tailed hawk ("Swoop")
COLORS:	red and white
CONFERENCE:	Pacific 12 Conference

HISTORY

The nickname for University of Utah athletic teams is the Utes. The school chose this name because the name Ute comes from the Native American Ute tribe, where the state's name originates. The Ute tribe granted the university permission to use their name.

The official mascot for the University of Utah is a costumed red-tailed hawk named Swoop. Swoop made his debut in 1996, after the Ute tribal council gave the university consent to use that particular mascot.

The University of Utah chose red and white to be the official school colors for their athletic teams. Unfortunately, there is no historical data explaining why those colors were chosen.

SCHOOL NAME: University of Virginia
NICKNAME: Cavaliers
MASCOT: cavalier
COLORS: orange and blue
CONFERENCE: Atlantic Coast Conference

HISTORY

In 1923, the University of Virginia (UVA) newspaper decided to hold a contest to choose a school alma mater and fight song. A senior by the name of John Morrow won the alma mater contest for selecting the song "Virginia, Hail All Hail," while junior Lawrence Haywood and sophomore Fulton Lewis Jr., won the fight song contest for respectively writing and composing "The Cavalier Song." Although neither was selected as the school's official alma mater and fight song, "The Cavalier Song" led to UVA adopting Cavaliers as the school's official nickname and mascot.

Orange and blue were not always the official school colors for UVA. Years ago, the school's athletic teams proudly wore the colors silver gray and cardinal red. Unfortunately, this color scheme did not stand out on muddy football fields. For this reason, in 1888, an on-campus student movement was organized to vote on a new school color. One of the students that attended this massive student movement was a UVA football player named Allan Potts. Allan came to the rally wearing an orange and blue scarf that he had acquired from Oxford University after spending a summer boating there. Orange and blue were adopted as the new school colors after a fellow student pulled Pott's scarf off his neck and waved it in the crowd, shouting, "How will this do?"

SCHOOL NAME: University of Washington
NICKNAME: Huskies
MASCOT: husky ("King Redoubt")
COLORS: purple and gold
CONFERENCE: Pacific 12 Conference

HISTORY

In November 1919, University of Washington (UW) athletic teams were known as the Sun Dodgers. That name was chosen by the student body out of protest when the college magazine of the same name was banned from the university. Unfortunately, this name was not conducive for a school that is located in the northwest. So in 1921, a committee was formed to come up with a new nickname. On February 3, 1922, Huskies was chosen by UW to be the new official school nickname. The name was selected by a committee of students, coaches, alumni, and businessmen. The announcement was made at halftime of the University of Washington versus Washington State University basketball game by Robert Ingram, who was the captain of the UW football team. When Ingram made his speech, large white placards were held up in the rooters section by senior letter winners that read, "The Husky stands for fight and tenacity, character and courage, endurance and willingness." Huskies was chosen by the committee because of Seattle's close proximity to the Alaska Frontier. The other finalist names were Wolves, Malamutes, Tyees, Vikings, Northmen, and Olympics.

UW chooses to use the Alaskan malamute husky as its official mascot because it is the largest and strongest of all the husky breeds. The first husky appeared at a university sporting event in 1922. That husky was adopted by the Sigma Alpha Epsilon fraternity, and his name was Frosty. Since that time, there have been quite a few husky replacements. Also, every succeeding mascot is given a different name.

In 1892, UW officially adopted its school colors at a student assembly. Initially, it was suggested by a patriotic group that the colors should be red, white, and blue, since the school is named after the first president of the United States. However, others opposed the idea, because they felt that the nation's colors should not be degraded for everyday use. That debate was finally put to rest when Ms. Frazier, who was an English instructor, stood up and read an excerpt from Lord Byron's *Destruction of Sennacherib,* "The Assyrian came down like the wolf on the fold, and his colors were gleaming in purple and gold; and the sheen of their spears was like stars on the sea, and the blue wave rolls nightly on deep Galilee." At the conclusion of the reading, it was the unanimous decision of the assembly to choose purple and gold as UW's official school colors.

SCHOOL NAME:	University of Wisconsin
NICKNAME:	Badgers
MASCOT:	badger ("Bucky")
COLORS:	cardinal and white
CONFERENCE:	Big Ten Conference

HISTORY

The state of Wisconsin was given the nickname the Badger State because of its association with lead miners back in the 1820s. Apparently, these prospectors, who came to the state looking for minerals, would tunnel burrows into hillsides in the winter and live like badgers to have shelter. Therefore, the University of Wisconsin decided to also use the state's name as their nickname.

Initially, the university used a real badger as its mascot, but the animal was too vicious. So in 1949, a student from the university's art department was asked by the homecoming chairman to make a papier-mâché badger head for the homecoming game. The head was worn by a university gymnast who was also a cheerleader. A contest was also established to name the new mascot. Buckingham U. Badger, or Bucky, was the winner. The name came from lyrics in a song that encouraged football players to "buck right through the line."

Legend has it that in the 1880s, the university briefly considered having a cardinal as its mascot. This could be the reason why cardinal became Wisconsin's official school color, with white used as the accent color.

SCHOOL NAME:	University of Wyoming
NICKNAME:	Cowboys
MASCOT:	pony ("Cowboy Joe")
COLORS:	brown and yellow
CONFERENCE:	Mountain West Conference

HISTORY

The official nickname for all athletic teams at the University of Wyoming (UW) is the Cowboys. Fred Bush, a 220-pound cowpuncher and member of the 1891 UW pickup football team, takes the credit for this happening. When Mr. Bush ran onto the football field with his fellow teammates (also ex-cowboys) wearing a checkered shirt and cowboy hat, someone yelled, "Hey, look at the cowboy!" UW students apparently took a liking to the name and selected it as the official nickname two years before the school played its first official football game.

With the UW Cowboy nickname now firmly in place, the school was now in search of a suitable mascot. As a result, it wasn't until 1950 that the Farthing family of Cheyenne put an end to this quest by donating a young pony to the university. The mascot was an instant success with the UW student body and was given the name Cowboy Joe.

Brown and yellow were chosen as the official school colors for UW back in 1895, which was the year of the university's first ever alumni banquet. Brown-eyed Susans, which are brown and yellow flowers native to Southwestern Wyoming, were the decorations used for this event. Fascinated by the flower's color and beauty, the UW Alumni Committee selected these colors to represent all the teams at UW.

SCHOOL NAME: Utah State University
NICKNAME: Aggies
MASCOT: bull ("Big Blue")
COLORS: navy blue and white
CONFERENCE: Mountain West Conference

HISTORY

In 1888, Utah State University (USU) was founded and was initially an agricultural school called the Agricultural College of Utah. As a result, when USU started competing in sports, the university chose Aggies as the nickname for its athletic teams because that name is short for "agriculture."

The official mascot for USU athletic teams is a bull named Big Blue. A bull first appeared at a football game in 1975, and a year later, it became the school's mascot. The name Big Blue was a term fans used in the 1960s when referencing USU teams because of the uniforms being blue. Consequently, USU decided to also give its mascot the same name. Originally, a real white bull painted blue would appear at all home game sporting events. However, when the bull damaged the football field, there was concern that the animal might damage the floor when Smith Spectrum stadium was built. USU then discontinued using a real animal and replaced it with a costumed bull.

In 1901, USU chose blue and white as the official school colors. Initially, royal blue was chosen. But by the 1920s, navy blue became the new color.

SCHOOL NAME: Vanderbilt University
NICKNAME: Commodores
MASCOT: commodore ("Mr. Commodore")
COLORS: black and gold
CONFERENCE: Southeastern Conference

HISTORY

The official nickname for all athletic teams at Vanderbilt University is the Commodores. The nickname stems from the founder of the university, Cornelius Vanderbilt, who was, of course, a member of the wealthy Vanderbilt family. Cornelius was called a commodore because he was regarded as a very aggressive businessman in the shipping industry. Ironically, he was never in the navy. Commodore was selected as the official school nickname by the Vanderbilt University student body in 1900.

A commodore, who goes by the name of Mr. Commodore, is the official mascot for Vanderbilt University.

The official school colors for Vanderbilt University are black and gold. Like the official nickname, this was also selected by the school's student body.

SCHOOL NAME:	Virginia Polytechnic Institute and State University
NICKNAME:	Hokies
MASCOT:	"HokieBird"
COLORS:	Chicago maroon and burnt orange
CONFERENCE:	Atlantic Coast Conference

HISTORY

When Virginia Agricultural and Mechanical College changed its name to Virginia Polytechnic Institute and State University (Virginia Tech) in 1896, the student body felt that it was also time for a new school cheer. A contest was held, and a senior by the name of O. M. Stull won first prize for what he called his "Hokie" yell. The Hokie yell, Stull explained, was a fictitious name he came up with as an attention getter. In time, all Tech athletic teams were nicknamed the Hokies.

Now that Virginia Tech had an official nickname, the school was in search of an official mascot. Because the name Hokie was associated with a yell, which resembled a birdcall, a Hokie bird became the obvious choice for a mascot.

A student body committee was also formed in 1896 to determine the official school colors for Virginia Tech. After thoroughly researching this subject, the committee unanimously decided to use the colors Chicago maroon and burnt orange when it was discovered that no other school at the time was using that color combination.

SCHOOL NAME: Wake Forest University
NICKNAME: Demon Deacons
MASCOT: "Demon Deacon"
COLORS: old gold and black
CONFERENCE: Atlantic Coast Conference

HISTORY

Wake Forest University, which was formally a Baptist school, has not always been known as the Demon Deacons. Back in 1895, they were called the Tigers. Over time, this common nickname lost interest with Wake Forest students and fans. In fact, by the 1920s, the college's athletic teams were referred to as the Baptist, or simply the Old Gold and Black. The new nickname was first introduced by Mayon Parker, who was the school's newspaper editor. Apparently, Mr. Parker felt that the athletic spirit that was now being generated around campus was in dire need of a new nickname. So in 1923, after Wake Forest defeated archrival Trinity College (now Duke University) in football, Parker referred to the team as Demon Deacons because of their devilish play and fighting spirit. The name was an instant hit with students, faculty, and fans alike. In time, Demon Deacons was adopted as Wake Forest University's official school nickname.

Wake Forest University's former nickname, the Tigers, explains why the school's colors are old gold and black.

SCHOOL NAME:	Washington State University
NICKNAME:	Cougars
MASCOT:	cougar ("Butch")
COLORS:	crimson and gray
CONFERENCE:	Pacific 12 Conference

HISTORY

On October 25, 1919, underdog Washington State College (now Washington State University) played a highly favored University of California at Berkley football team in what was only Coach Gus Welch of Washington State College's (WSC) second game. After upsetting a very good Berkley team, a California Bay area sportswriter said that the Pacific Northwest team "played like cougars." When the student body at WSC got wind of this, the name Cougars was an instant success. As a result, on October 28, 1919, WSC adopted Cougars as the official nickname and mascot for all their athletic teams.

Eight years after WSC adopted Cougars as their official nickname and mascot, WSC got its first live cougar mascot. At halftime of the WSC versus University of Idaho homecoming football game, which was played on November 11, 1927, Washington state governor Roland H. Hartley did the honors of presenting WSC with their first live mascot. Initially, WSC students named their cougar Governor Hartley, in honor of its donor. However, after he graciously declined the offer, the governor suggested that the school rename their mascot Butch. This was short for Herbert L. "Butch" Meeker, who was WSC's football hero of the day. The name fared well with WSC students, and like his predecessor, the cougar was given the name Butch.

Years ago, prior to Washington State University being named Washington State College, the school was known as Washington Agricultural College (WAC). To add, the official school colors for WAC were pink and blue. Legend has it that there are two possible reasons why WAC chose these unusual colors.

The first reason has to do with the nickname given to the college's first building, the Crib, which was a humorous name derived from "the Cradle of Learning." The second has to do with the beautiful sunsets that are very common, particularly in the winter, at WAC. The sun would cast a pretty pink glow over the rolling hills and campus buildings and would take on a breathtaking shade of blue.

Although the legends of the pink and blue were quite appealing to the ear, WAC's president viewed these colors as being harsh on the eyes. So in 1900, he appointed a committee to select new school colors. The three color combinations of pink and blue, blue and white, and crimson and gray were up for debate. Crimson and gray were selected as the official school colors to represent the athletic teams at WAC.

SCHOOL NAME:	West Virginia University
NICKNAME:	Mountaineers
MASCOT:	mountaineer
COLORS:	old gold and blue
CONFERENCE:	Big 12 Conference

HISTORY

Since West Virginia is known as the Mountain State, all West Virginians are simply called Mountaineers. For this reason, the Mountaineer was adopted as the official nickname and mascot for West Virginia University (WVU).

WVU selected old gold and blue as their official school colors to be the same as the West Virginia state flag.

SCHOOL NAME: Western Kentucky University
NICKNAME: Hilltoppers
MASCOT: furry blob ("Big Red")
COLORS: red and white
CONFERENCE: Conference USA

HISTORY

The official nickname for Western Kentucky University's (WKU) athletic teams is the Hilltoppers. That name was chosen because the school's campus sits on top of a 232-foot hill that overlooks the Barren River, which runs through the town of Bowling Green.

The mascot for WKU athletic teams is Big Red. Big Red represents the spirit of WKU and was created in 1979 by a WKU student named Ralph Cary. The university asked Mr. Cary to create a mascot to replace the red towels that were waived by WKU fans to show their school spirit. Cary's decision to create a furry blob as the mascot was due to the fact that he wanted to stay as far away as possible from the hillbilly stereotype of Kentuckians.

The official school colors of WKU's athletic teams are red and white. Unfortunately, there is no historical data explaining why those colors were chosen.

SCHOOL NAME: Western Michigan University
NICKNAME: Broncos
MASCOT: bronco ("Buster")
COLORS: brown and gold
CONFERENCE: Mid-American Conference

HISTORY

Western Michigan University (WMU) athletic teams used to be called the Hilltoppers. That name was coined because of the location of the school, which was on top of Prospect Hill. The Bronco nickname was adopted in 1939 by assistant football coach John Gill. The name was changed to avoid confusion with Western Kentucky and Marquette, which also used the Hilltoppers name.

In 1981, WMU student body held a contest to select the official name of the school's mascot. At the conclusion of that contest, Buster was the chosen name. Then in 1988, Buster Bronco was born and hired by the WMU athletic department to be the school's first masqueraded bronco mascot.

In 1905, Dwight Waldo, who was WMU's first president, chose brown and gold to be the school's official colors. He made the decision after his secretary suggested that he go with that color combination, which follows the pattern of the brown-eyed Susan flower. This flower is known for its dark brown center surrounded by vivid yellow petals.

SCHOOL TRIVIA QUESTIONS

1. What college uses a color to identify its nickname and does not have a mascot to represent its athletic teams? (see page 60)

2. Name the colleges who's school colors were derived from the state flag associated with the state where the school is located? (see pages 85, 100, 112 and 148)

3. What are the only two schools that use Cherry Red as one of their colors? (see pages 63 and 114)

4. What college does not have a mascot? (see page 13)

5. What two colleges have the same mascot and school colors? (see pages 80 and 81)

6. Name the colleges that have school colors derived from other colleges. (see pages 10, 48, 49, 59, 80, 87, 95 and 108)

7. How many colleges have a bird as a mascot? (read and you will find the answer)

Printed in the United States
By Bookmasters